HIGHEST MOUNTAIN SMALLEST STAR

A PICTORIAL COMPENDIUM OF NATURAL WONDERS

ILLUSTRATED BY PAGE TSOU

WRITTEN BY KATE BAKER

B P P

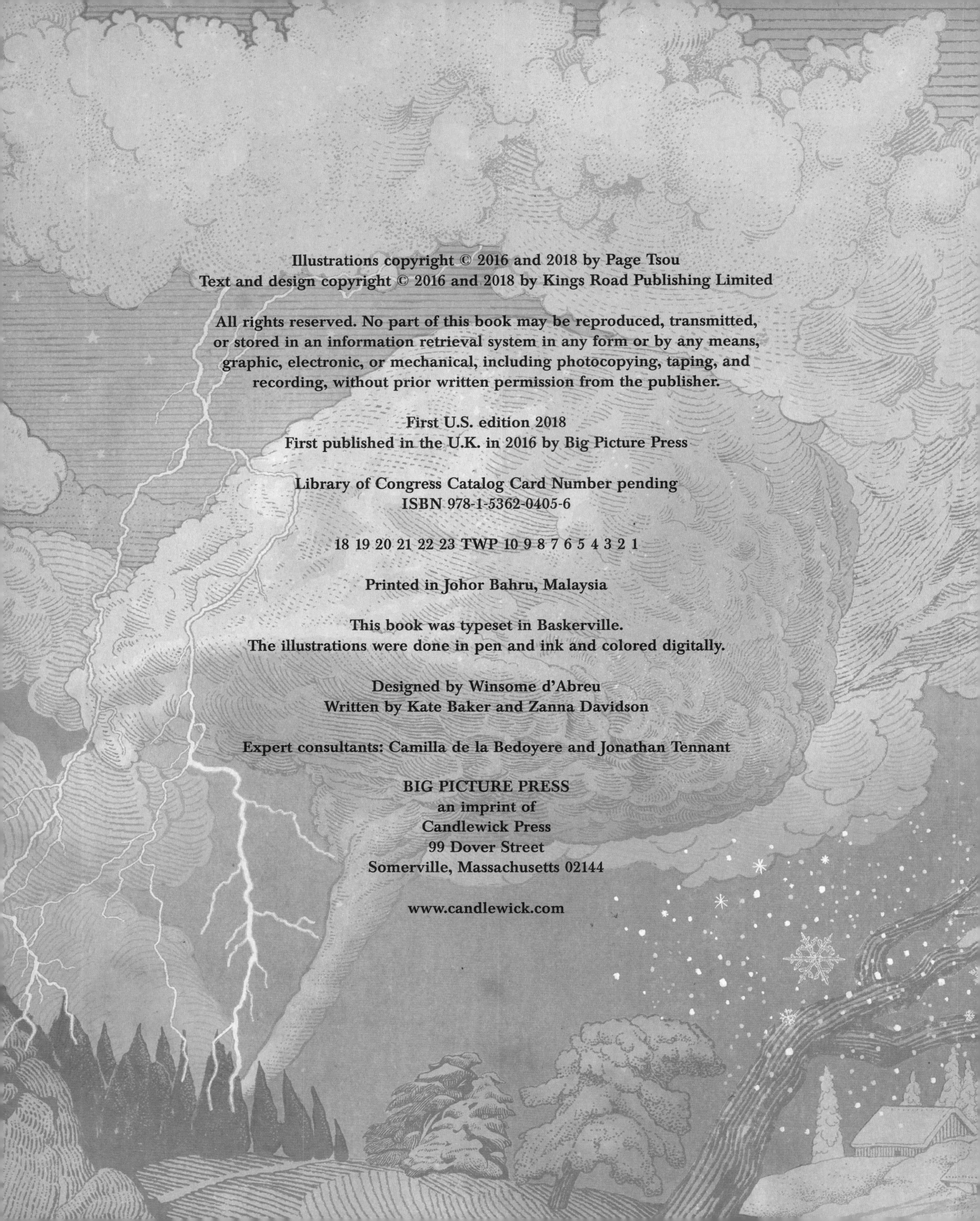

Illustrations copyright © 2016 and 2018 by Page Tsou
Text and design copyright © 2016 and 2018 by Kings Road Publishing Limited

First U.S. edition 2018
First published in the U.K. in 2016 by Big Picture Press

Library of Congress Catalog Card Number pending
ISBN 978-1-5362-0405-6

18 19 20 21 22 23 TWP 10 9 8 7 6 5 4 3 2 1

Printed in Johor Bahru, Malaysia

This book was typeset in Baskerville.
The illustrations were done in pen and ink and colored digitally.

Designed by Winsome d'Abreu
Written by Kate Baker and Zanna Davidson

Expert consultants: Camilla de la Bedoyere and Jonathan Tennant

BIG PICTURE PRESS
an imprint of
Candlewick Press
99 Dover Street
Somerville, Massachusetts 02144

www.candlewick.com

HIGHEST
MOUNTAIN
SMALLEST
STAR

A PICTORIAL COMPENDIUM
OF NATURAL WONDERS

ILLUSTRATED BY PAGE TSOU
WRITTEN BY KATE BAKER

B P P

Contents

Just how tall is the highest mountain on the planet? What are the tallest structures humans have built throughout history? Which creature had the most powerful bite? What is the fastest animal?

Here, you can discover how big some of the largest dinosaurs were, and you can find out how big the largest mammals are right now. Find out which birds migrate the farthest and which fish swim in the deepest parts of the ocean. Discover the tiniest creatures we've found so far and how far away scientists think the edge of the universe is.

Within these pages you will find a wealth of information that will help you to understand exactly how heavy, how strong, how small, and how tall things really are.

Some of the Largest Dinosaurs
and the Largest Pterosaur

The ancient reptiles shown here are some of the longest and heaviest creatures to ever walk the Earth. In some cases, only incomplete remains have been found, so the sizes given here are scientists' best estimates and may be open to debate.

Large HERBIVORES

❶ Argentinosaurus huinculensis Weight: More than 55 tons/50 metric tons • Length: 98 ft./30 m • Lived: Argentina, 97–94 mya (million years ago). Currently holds the record for being the heaviest and longest land animal ever.

❷ Turiasaurus riodevensis Weight: 55 tons/50 metric tons • Length: 98 ft./30 m • Lived: Western Europe, 150–140 mya

❸ Brachiosaurus altithorax Weight: 39 tons/35 metric tons • Length: 72 ft./22 m • Lived: North America, 157–145 mya

❹ Paralititan stromeri Weight: 22 tons/20 metric tons • Length: 66 ft./20 m • Lived: Egypt, 98–93 mya

❺ Dreadnoughtus schrani Weight: 28 tons/25 metric tons • Length: 82 ft./25 m • Lived: Argentina, 84–66 mya

Large **CARNIVORES**

6 ***Spinosaurus aegyptiacus*** Weight: 11 tons/ 10 metric tons • Length: 46 ft./14 m • Lived: North Africa, 112–97 mya

7 ***Carcharodontosaurus saharicus*** Weight: 6½ tons/6 metric tons • Length: 39 ft./12 m • Lived: North Africa, 100–94 mya

8 ***Giganotosaurus carolinii*** Weight: 9 tons/8 metric tons • Length: 43 ft./13 m • Lived: South America, 99–97 mya

9 ***Tyrannosaurus rex*** Weight: 6½ tons/6 metric tons • Length: 39 ft./12 m • Lived: North America, 68–66 mya

10 ***Mapusaurus roseae*** Weight: 5½ tons/5 metric tons • Length: 39 ft./12 m • Lived: South America, 100–93 mya

Large **PTEROSAUR**

11 ***Quetzalcoatlus northropi*** Weight: 550 lbs./ 250 kg • Wingspan: 36 ft./11 m • Lived: North America, 72–66 mya

13

*T*he majestic blue whale is the largest animal ever to have lived. Its tongue alone weighs as much as an elephant, its heart as much as a small car. On land, the mighty African elephant is the largest animal, the giraffe the tallest.

*L*iving in the deepest depths of the ocean are species that reach gigantic proportions, from the giant squid, which grows large enough to battle sperm whales, to the giant isopod, a cousin of the wood louse that can grow up to eight times the size of its shallow-water relatives.

A Malayan tapir weighs the same as a motorcycle.

❶ **Blue whale** Up to 200 tons/180 metric tons, 98 ft./30 m long (the longest and loudest animal, with vocalizations of more than 180 decibels)

❷ **Fin whale** Up to 70 tons/63.5 metric tons, 88 ft./26.8 m long (one of the fastest whales, capable of speeds up to 23 mph/37 kmh)

❸ **Sperm whale** Up to 45 tons/40 metric tons, up to 59 ft./17 m long

❹ **Whale shark** Up to 20 tons/18 metric tons, 33 ft./10 m long

❺ **Orca** Up to 9 tons/8 metric tons

❻ **Basking shark** Up to 7½ tons/7 metric tons, 33 ft./10 m long

❼ **West Indian manatee** Up to 3,300 lbs./1.5 metric tons, 15 ft./4.5 m long

❽ **Beluga whale** Up to 2,900 lbs./1.3 metric tons, 17 ft./5.3 m long

ANIMALS *on land...*

❶ **African elephant**
Up to 7 tons/6.3 metric tons, 13 ft./4 m tall

❷ **Common hippopotamus**
Up to 4 tons/3.6 metric tons, 14 ft./4.2 m long

❸ **Saltwater crocodile**
Up to 1,000 lbs./454 kg, 16 ft./5 m long

❹ **Shire horse**
Up to 2,000 lbs./900 kg, 6 ft./1.8 m tall

❺ **White rhinoceros**
Up to 4 tons/3.6 metric tons, 14 ft./4.2 m long

❻ **Grévy's zebra**
Up to 990 lbs./450 kg, 5 ft./1.5 m tall

❼ **Eurasian moose**
Up to 1,800 lbs./816 kg, 6½ ft./2 m tall

❽ **Elephant seal**
Up to 4½ tons/4 metric tons, 20 ft./6 m long

❾ **Masai giraffe**
Up to 2,800 lbs./1.27 metric tons, 20 ft./6 m tall

❿ **Water buffalo**
Up to 2,600 lbs./1.2 metric tons, 9 ft./2.7 m long

⓫ **American bison**
Up to 2,200 lbs./1 metric ton, 11½ ft./3.5 m long

⓬ **Bactrian camel**
Up to 1,800 lbs./816 kg, 7 ft./2.1 m tall

⓭ **Siberian tiger**
Up to 660 lbs./300 kg, 11 ft./3.3 m long

⓮ **Polar bear**
Up to 1,600 lbs./725 kg, 8 ft./2.4 m long

⓯ **Malay tapir**
Up to 800 lbs./363 kg, 3½ ft./1.1 m tall

⓰ **Brown bear**
Up to 700 lbs./317 kg, 8 ft./2.4 m long

⓱ **Eastern lowland gorilla**
Up to 440 lbs./199 kg, 5½ ft./1.7 m tall

and in the ocean

❾ **Lion's mane jellyfish**
Up to 2,200 lbs./1 metric ton,
197 ft./60 m long, 6½ ft./2 m wide

❿ **Giant squid**
Up to 1 ton/907 kg, 43 ft./13 m
long

⓫ **Giant manta ray**
Up to 4,400 lbs./2 metric tons,
23 ft./7 m wide

⓬ **Sunflower sea star**
Up to 11 lbs./5 kg, 3 ft./1 m
diameter

⓭ **Giant isopod**
Up to 3½ lbs./1.7 kg, 30 in./76 cm
long

⓮ **Japanese spider crab**
Up to 40 lbs./18 kg, 13 ft./4 m claw
to claw

Among the World's Largest Butterflies

1. **Queen Alexandra's birdwing** (*Ornithoptera alexandrae*) Wingspan: 11 in./27 cm

2. **Goliath birdwing** (*Ornithoptera goliath*) Wingspan: 9 in./23 cm

3. **African giant swallowtail** (*Papilio antimachus*) Wingspan: 9 in./23 cm

4. **Buru opalescent birdwing** (*Troides prattorum*) Wingspan: 6–7 in./15–17 cm

5. **Palawan birdwing** (*Trogonoptera trojana*) Wingspan: 7 in./18 cm

6. **Rippon's birdwing** (*Troides hypolitus*) Wingspan: 8 in./20 cm

7. **Chimaera birdwing** (*Ornithoptera chimaera*) Wingspan: 6 in./16 cm

8. **Wallace's golden birdwing** (*Ornithoptera croesus lydius*) Wingspan: 8 in./20 cm

9. **Magellan birdwing** (*Troides magellanus*) Wingspan: 7 in./18 cm

10. **Queen Victoria's birdwing** (*Ornithoptera victoriae*) Wingspan: 7 in./18 cm

Among the World's Largest Bugs

11. **Giant burrowing cockroach** (*Macropanesthia rhinoceros*) 3 in./8 cm long

12. **Hercules beetle** (*Dynastes hercules*) 7 in./18 cm long

13. **Titan beetle** (*Titanus giganteus*) 6½ in./17 cm long

14. **Egyptian giant camel spider** (*Galeodes arabs*) 6 in./15 cm long (including legs)

15. **Giant walking stick insect** (*Phryganistria chinensis*) 24 in./62 cm long — the world's longest insect

16. **Giant water bug** (*Lethocerus americanus*) 4 in./10 cm long, wingspan 8½ in./22 cm

17. **Elephant beetle** (*Megasoma elephas*) 5 in./13 cm long (with its horn raised)

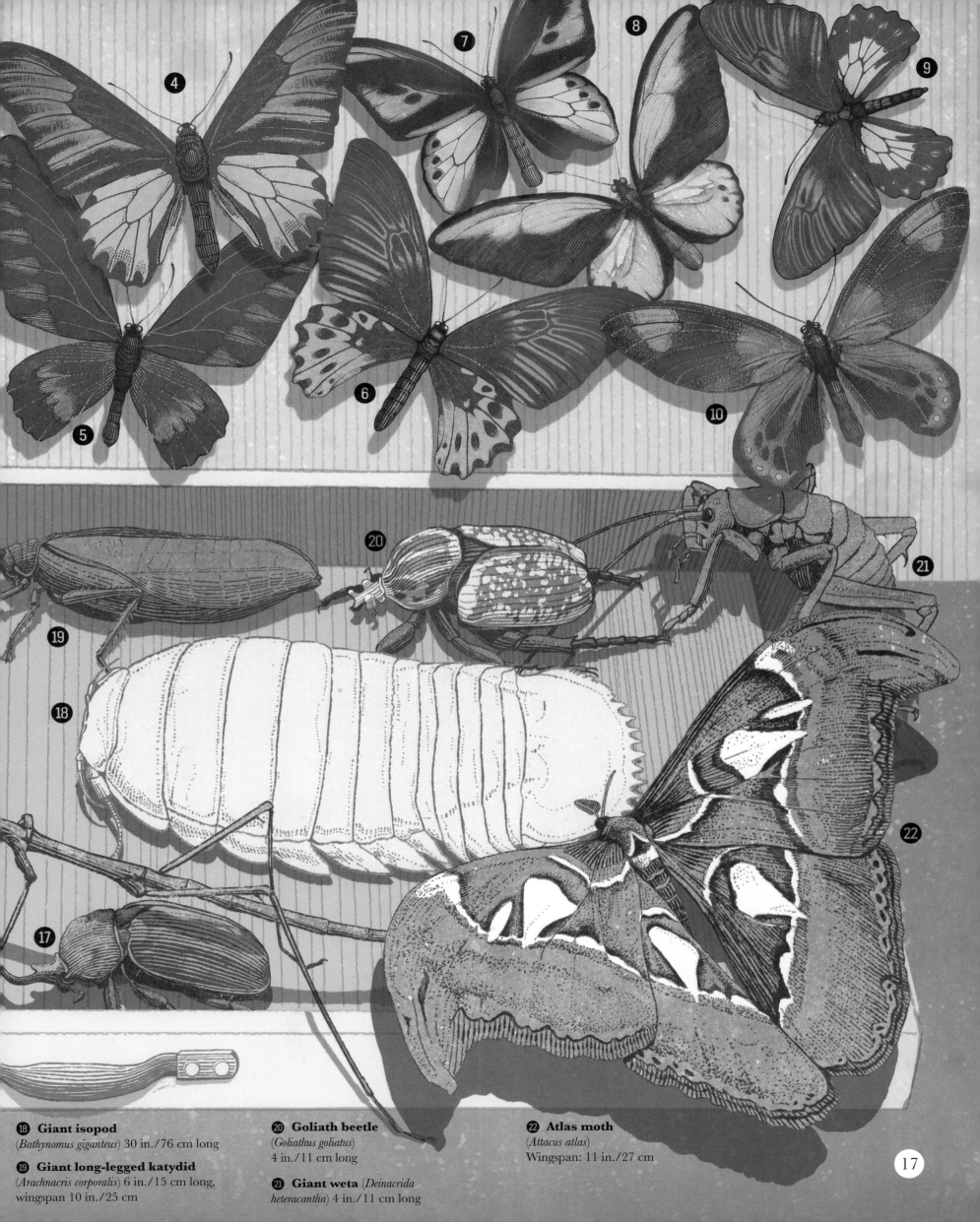

18 **Giant isopod**
(*Bathynomus giganteus*) 30 in./76 cm long

19 **Giant long-legged katydid**
(*Arachnacris corporalis*) 6 in./15 cm long,
wingspan 10 in./25 cm

20 **Goliath beetle**
(*Goliathus goliatus*)
4 in./11 cm long

21 **Giant weta** (*Deinacrida
heteracantha*) 4 in./11 cm long

22 **Atlas moth**
(*Attacus atlas*)
Wingspan: 11 in./27 cm

THE TALLEST, LARGEST, WIDEST, AND OLDEST LIVING TREES

Tallest tree:
A **coast redwood** (*Sequoia sempervirens*) named Hyperion in Redwood National Park, California, which stands 379 feet 4 inches / 115.6 meters tall in Redwood National Park, California.

Oldest known clonal colony tree: Pando, or the Trembling Giant, an enormous grove of **quaking aspen** (*Populus tremuloides*) in Fishlake National Forest, Utah; estimated to be 80,000 years old

Oldest non-clonal tree:
A **Great Basin bristlecone pine** (*Pinus longaeva*) in the White Mountains of California; more than 5,065 years old

Oldest known vegetatively cloned tree: Old Tjikko, a **Norway spruce** (*Picea abies*) in Fulufjället National Park, Sweden; 9,550 years old

Largest tree (by volume): **A giant sequoia** (*Sequoiadendron giganteum*) known as General Sherman in Sequoia National Park, California; calculated to be 52,513 cubic feet/1,487 cubic meters.

Widest tree: A **Montezuma cypress** (*Taxodium mucronatum*) known as the Árbol del Tule in Oaxaca, Mexico; 38 feet/11.6 meters in diameter

Largest leaves

Raphia palm (*Raphia regalis*): leaves up to 82 ft./25 m long

Largest seeds

Coconut (*Cocos nucifera*): 3 lbs./1.4 kg, 6 in./15 cm long

Coco de mer (*Lodoicea maldivica*): up to 55 lbs./125 kg

The Solar System

Jupiter

Our solar system is made up of the sun and the planets that orbit it. It also includes at least 146 moons, as well as comets, asteroids, minor planets, space rocks, dust, and gas.

Sun

Mercury Venus Earth Mars

Asteroid Belt

Mercury
Radius: 1,516 mi./ 2,440 km
Distance from the sun: 36 million mi./58 million km

Venus
Radius: 3,760 mi./ 6,052 km
Distance from the sun: 67 million mi./108 million km

Earth
Radius: 3,959 mi./ 6,371 km
Distance from the sun: 93 million mi./150 million km

Mars
Radius: 2,106 mi./ 3,390 km
Distance from the sun: 142 million mi./228 million km

Jupiter
Radius: 43,441 mi./69,911 km
Distance from the sun: 484 million mi./778.3 million km

Between Mars and Jupiter lies the asteroid belt, which is filled with space rocks that range in diameter from 329 miles/530 kilometers to less than 33 feet/10 meters. These rocks are left over from the formation of our solar system, about 4.6 billion years ago.

Planetary orbits around the sun

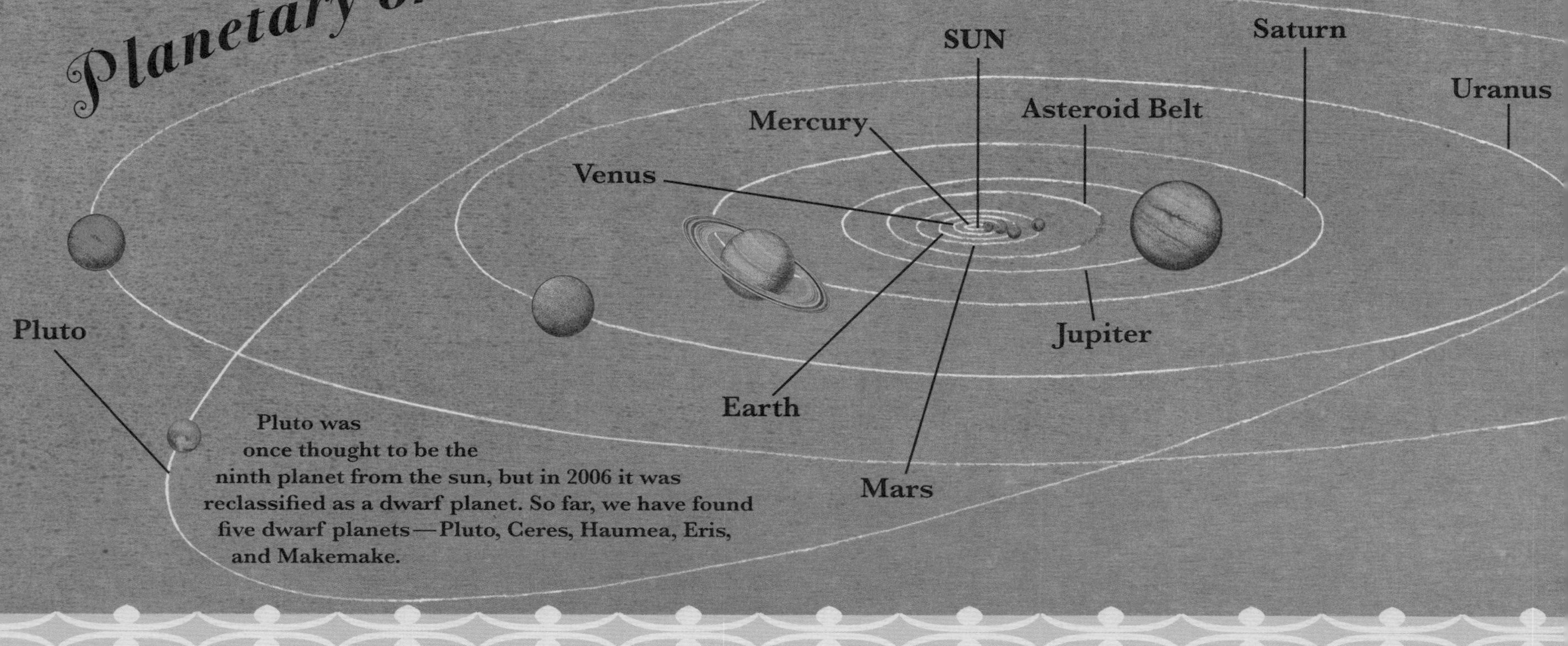

SUN

Saturn

Uranus

Mercury

Asteroid Belt

Venus

Jupiter

Pluto

Earth

Mars

Pluto was once thought to be the ninth planet from the sun, but in 2006 it was reclassified as a dwarf planet. So far, we have found five dwarf planets—Pluto, Ceres, Haumea, Eris, and Makemake.

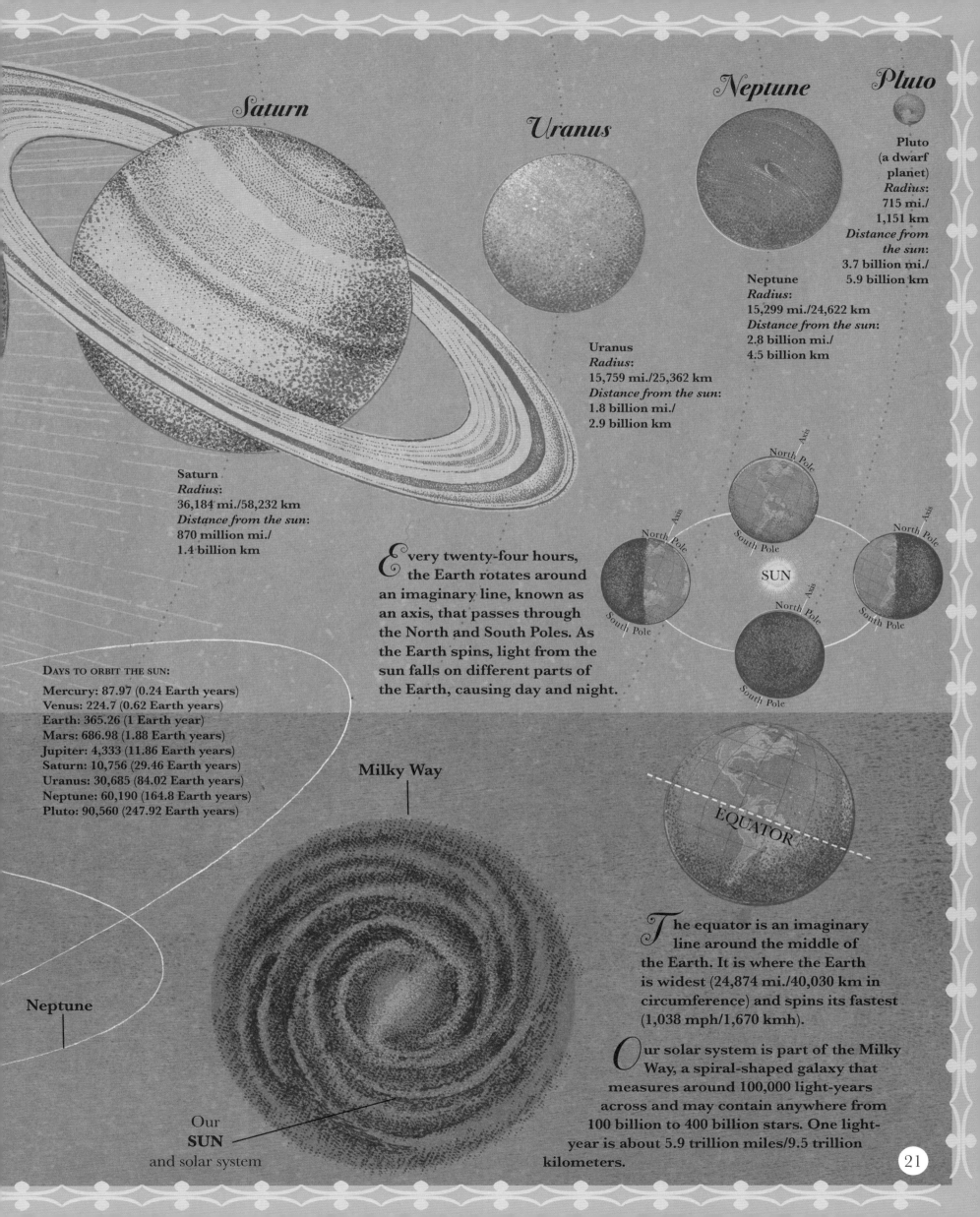

Saturn

Uranus

Neptune

Pluto

Pluto
(a dwarf
planet)
Radius:
715 mi./
1,151 km
*Distance from
the sun:*
3.7 billion mi./
5.9 billion km

Neptune
Radius:
15,299 mi./24,622 km
Distance from the sun:
2.8 billion mi./
4.5 billion km

Uranus
Radius:
15,759 mi./25,362 km
Distance from the sun:
1.8 billion mi./
2.9 billion km

Saturn
Radius:
36,184 mi./58,232 km
Distance from the sun:
870 million mi./
1.4 billion km

North Pole
Axis

North Pole
Axis

South Pole

SUN

North Pole
Axis

South Pole

North Pole

South Pole

North Pole

South Pole

*E*very twenty-four hours,
the Earth rotates around
an imaginary line, known as
an axis, that passes through
the North and South Poles. As
the Earth spins, light from the
sun falls on different parts of
the Earth, causing day and night.

DAYS TO ORBIT THE SUN:

Mercury: 87.97 (0.24 Earth years)
Venus: 224.7 (0.62 Earth years)
Earth: 365.26 (1 Earth year)
Mars: 686.98 (1.88 Earth years)
Jupiter: 4,333 (11.86 Earth years)
Saturn: 10,756 (29.46 Earth years)
Uranus: 30,685 (84.02 Earth years)
Neptune: 60,190 (164.8 Earth years)
Pluto: 90,560 (247.92 Earth years)

Milky Way

Neptune

EQUATOR

*T*he equator is an imaginary
line around the middle of
the Earth. It is where the Earth
is widest (24,874 mi./40,030 km in
circumference) and spins its fastest
(1,038 mph/1,670 kmh).

Our
SUN
and solar system

*O*ur solar system is part of the Milky
Way, a spiral-shaped galaxy that
measures around 100,000 light-years
across and may contain anywhere from
100 billion to 400 billion stars. One light-
year is about 5.9 trillion miles/9.5 trillion
kilometers.

From the Earth to the MOON

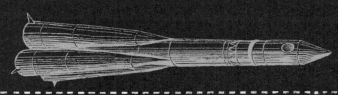

3,317 days
nonstop on foot

166 days
nonstop by car

Around 3 days
by rocket

Around 240,000 miles to the Moon

The moon is believed to have formed after a massive collision between the Earth and an asteroid around 4.5 billion years ago. The debris from the impact came together to form the moon. At the time of its formation, the moon was much closer to the Earth — 14,000 miles/22,500 kilometers away, compared to 240,000 miles/386,000 kilometers on average today.

Earth's gravitational force keeps the moon in orbit, but the moon also exerts gravitational force on the Earth. The moon's gravity causes Earth's tides; has slowed Earth's rotation, resulting in our twenty-four-hour day; and keeps Earth's axis tilted between 22.1 and 24.5 degrees, even over thousands of years, which gives us our seasons. But the moon's gravitational force on the Earth is decreasing

by infinitesimal amounts as its distance from the Earth continues to increase — at the rate of 1½ inches/4 centimeters per year, about the same speed at which our fingernails grow.

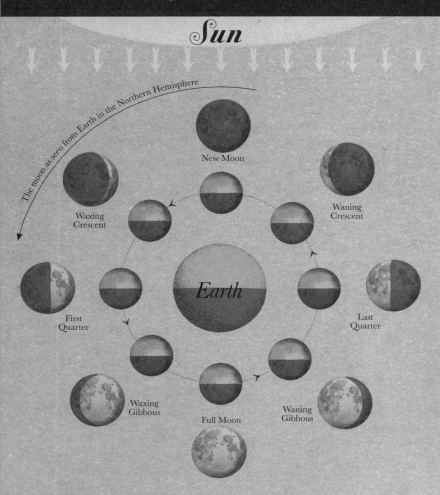

Sun

The moon as seen from Earth in the Northern Hemisphere

New Moon

Waxing Crescent

Waning Crescent

Earth

First Quarter

Last Quarter

Waxing Gibbous

Full Moon

Waning Gibbous

It takes 27.3 days for the moon to orbit the Earth, and the appearance of the moon changes over the cycle. These changes are known as the phases of the moon. Each phase depends on the amount of the moon you can see from Earth as it is lit up by the sun. This amount changes each day according to the moon's position in relation to the Earth and the sun.

MOON RABBIT

For thousands of years, humans have looked up at the moon and imagined a host of characters gazing back at them. Chinese legends have long told of a curious rabbit that lives on the surface of the moon. The Moon Rabbit—also known as the Jade Rabbit or the Gold Rabbit—is the faithful companion to the beautiful goddess Chang'e, who floated to the moon after she accidentally drank too much of an immortality potion. Together they live in the Moon Palace, and the rabbit spends its days pounding the elixir of life in a mortar.

In Japanese folklore, the Moon Rabbit is known as Tsuki no Usagi, and instead of the elixir of life, it makes rice cakes. Cree tradition tells of a rabbit that once longed to ride to the moon. He asked birds large and small to help him, but all refused, until one day a crane agreed to take him. The rabbit clung on so tightly to the crane's legs that they became elongated—just as cranes' legs are to this day.

Scientists will tell you that the mysterious patterns and shapes are in fact produced by the contours of the surface of the moon. The lighter areas are the mountains. The dark areas are the maria (Latin for "seas")—vast craters filled with volcanic rock.

In December 2013, China landed a lunar rover named Yutu or "Jade Rabbit" on the moon.

Sun

Sun

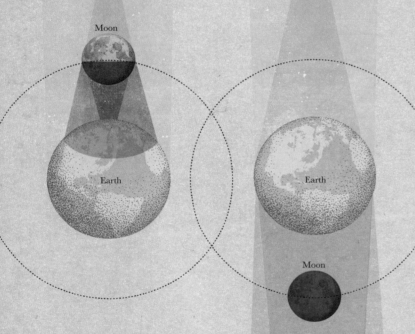

Moon

Earth

Earth

Moon

SOLAR ECLIPSE

A solar eclipse occurs when the moon is in new moon phase and passes between the Earth and the sun, causing it to cast a shadow over the Earth. The moon's diameter is four hundred times less than the sun's, but the moon also happens to be about four hundred times closer to Earth than the sun is. As a result, it appears in our sky to be the same size as the sun and is therefore able to block it out.

LUNAR ECLIPSE

A lunar eclipse happens when the moon passes directly behind the Earth into its umbra (shadow), which casts the moon into an eerie darkness. For a total lunar eclipse, the sun, Earth, and full moon need to be exactly or very closely aligned, with Earth in the middle. In the current era, the moon is at the perfect distance for Earth's shadow to cover the moon. Billions of years from now, that won't be the case.

The MOON is around 240,000 mi./ 384,400 km from the Earth.

201,700 mi./ 324,600 km: distance of asteroid 2005 YU55's Earth flyby, November 2011

Luna 2: the first spacecraft to reach the moon

Neil Armstrong: the first person to walk on the moon

31,000 mi./50,000 km: END OF MAGNETOSPHERE

6,200 mi./10,000 km: END OF EXOSPHERE

22,000 mi./ 36,000 km: communications satellite

2,000 km

1,031 mi./1,660 km: maximum altitude in space reached by a dog

373 mi./600 km: END OF THERMOSPHERE

Approx. 240 mi./400km: International Space Station

203 mi./327 km: maximum altitude reached by the first person in space, Yuri Gagarin, in 1961

60–200 mi./97–322 km: AURORA BOREALIS

53 mi./85 km: END OF MESOSPHERE

31 mi./50 km: END OF STRATOSPHERE

25.7 mi./ 41.4 km: highest skydive

13.6 mi./21.9 km: maximum altitude reached by the first supersonic aircraft, Bell X-1

69,000 ft./21 km: highest hot-air balloon flight

6.8 mi./11 km: commercial aircraft cruising altitude

4–12 mi./6–20 km: END OF TROPOSPHERE

37,000 ft./11.2 km: highest-flying bird (Rüppell's griffon vulture)

10 ft./3 m: altitude of the first powered, sustained, and controlled airplane flight (Orville Wright, December 1903)

29,029 ft./8,848 m: height of the highest mountain on Earth, Mount Everest

EARTH

23

280,000 km
260,000 km
240,000 km
220,000 km
180,000 km
160,000 km
140,000 km
120,000 km
90,000 km
80,000 km
70,000 km
60,000 km
40,000 km
30,000 km
20,000 km
8,000 km
6,000 km
4,000 km
1,900 km
1,800 km
1,700 km
1,600 km
1,500 km
1,400 km
1,300 km
1,200 km
1,100 km
900 km
800 km
700 km
600 km
500 km
400 km
300 km
200 km

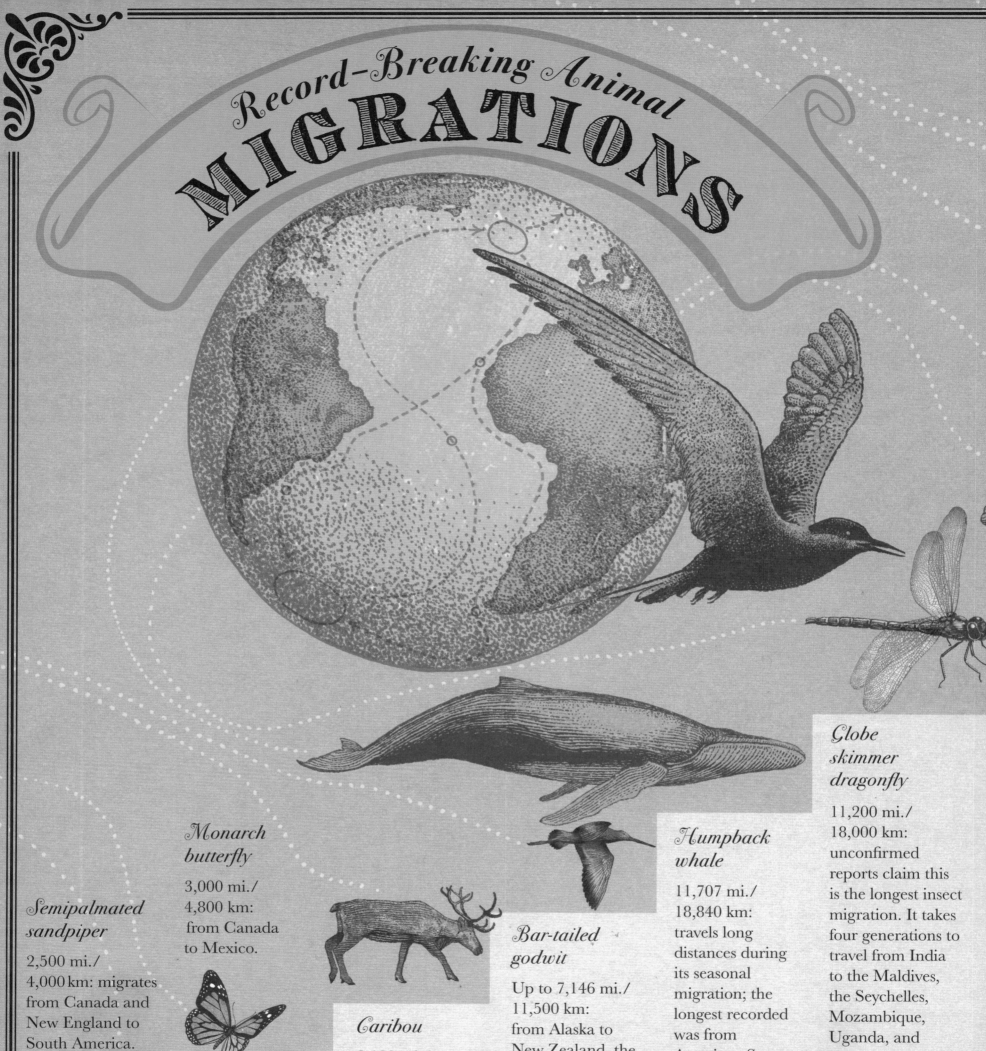

Record-Breaking Animal
MIGRATIONS

Semipalmated sandpiper

2,500 mi./ 4,000 km: migrates from Canada and New England to South America.

Monarch butterfly

3,000 mi./ 4,800 km: from Canada to Mexico.

Caribou

3,100 mi./ 5,000 km: travels 40 mi./ 64 km in a day.

Bar-tailed godwit

Up to 7,146 mi./ 11,500 km: from Alaska to New Zealand, the longest nonstop flight of any bird.

Humpback whale

11,707 mi./ 18,840 km: travels long distances during its seasonal migration; the longest recorded was from American Samoa to Antarctica.

Globe skimmer dragonfly

11,200 mi./ 18,000 km: unconfirmed reports claim this is the longest insect migration. It takes four generations to travel from India to the Maldives, the Seychelles, Mozambique, Uganda, and back again.

Arctic tern

60,000 mi./ 96,000 km: the longest of all animal migrations, from the Arctic Circle to the Antarctic region and back again.

Sooty shearwater

40,000 mi./ 64,000 km: travels between New Zealand and the North Pacific, covering as many as 620 mi./ 1,000 km in a day.

In medieval times, it was thought that barnacle geese grew on trees.

Tuna

25,000 mi./ 40,000 km: makes three Pacific Ocean crossings between the U.S. and Japan over twenty months.

Gray whale

14,000 mi./ 22,500 km: its annual round-trip from tropical to colder waters is the longest of any mammal.

Northern elephant seal

13,000 mi./ 21,000 km: migrates the vast distance between California and Alaska each year.

Leatherback sea turtle

12,000 mi./ 20,000 km: the longest migration recorded began in Indonesia and ended in Oregon.

Aristotle

Winter

Summer

Before animal migration was fully understood, people had some interesting explanations for the seasonal movement of birds. For centuries, it was widely believed that birds spent the winter hiding in mud at the bottom of lakes and ponds. In ancient Greece, Aristotle declared that winter robins were transformed into redstarts during the summer months and that blackcaps turned into garden warblers. During the Middle Ages, the sudden appearance of barnacle geese gave rise to the belief that they grew from the black-and-white shells of barnacles or like fruit from a tree.

25

Some of the HIGHEST MOUNTAINS

Of the five highest mountain peaks, four are in the Himalayas, the highest mountain range in the world. (Mountain height is measured as meters/feet above sea level.) The Himalayas span five countries—Nepal, India, Bhutan, China, and Pakistan. The list below continues with some of the most famous and notable mountains in the world, if not the tallest.

❶ *Mount Everest, Himalayas, Asia*—29,029 ft./8,848 m

❷ *K2, Karakoram, Asia*—28,251 ft./8,611 m

❸ *Kanchenjunga, Himalayas, Asia*—28,169 ft./8,586 m

❹ *Lhotse, Himalayas, Asia*—27,940 ft./8,516 m

❺ *Makalu, Himalayas, Asia*—27,762 ft./8,462 m

❻ *Mount Aconcagua, Andes, South America*—22,841 ft./6,962 m, highest mountain in the Western Hemisphere

❼ *Ojos del Salado, South America*—22,615 ft./6,893 m

❽ *Denali, Alaska Range, North America*—20,308 ft./6,191 m, highest mountain in North America

❾ *Mount Logan, Saint Elias Mountains, North America*—19,550 ft./5,990 m

❿ *Cotopaxi, Andes, South America*—19,386 ft./5,909 m

⓫ *Kilimanjaro, Africa*—19,340 ft./5,895 m, highest mountain in Africa

⓬ *Mount Elbrus, Caucasus, Europe*—18,510 ft./5,642 m, highest peak of the Caucasus Mountains

⓭ *Pico de Orizaba, Cordillera Neovolcanica, North America*—18,251 ft./5,563 m

⓮ *Popocatépetl, Cordillera Neovolcanica, North America*—17,802 ft./5,426 m

⓯ *Dykh-Tau, Caucasus, Europe*—17,073 ft./5,204 m

⓰ *Mount Kenya, Africa*—17,057 ft./5,199 m

⓱ *Great Ararat, Asia*—16,945 ft./5,165 m

⓲ *Vinson Massif, Ellsworth Mountains, Antarctica*—16,066 ft./4,897 m, highest peak in Antarctica

⓳ *Puncak Jaya, Maoke Range, Oceania*—16,024 ft./4,884 m

⓴ *Mont Blanc, Alps, Europe*—15,771 ft./4,807 m

㉑ *Matterhorn, Alps, Europe*—14,692 ft./4,478 m

㉒ *Mauna Kea, Hawaii, North America*—13,796 ft./4,205 m, the tallest mountain in the world when measured from its seafloor base to summit.

㉓ *Mount Toubkal, High Atlas, Africa*—13,665 ft./4,165 m, highest of the Atlas Mountains

㉔ *Mount Kinabalu, Asia*—13,455 ft./4,101 m, highest mountain in Borneo

㉕ *Mount Fuji, Asia*—12,388 ft./3,776 m, highest mountain in Japan

㉖ *Mount Cook, Southern Alps, Oceania*—12,218 ft./3,724 m, highest point in New Zealand

㉗ *Mount Olympus, Greek-Albanian Ranges, Europe*—9,570 ft./2,917 m, highest mountain in Greece and home of the gods, according to Greek mythology

㉘ *Mount Sinai, Africa*—7,497 ft./2,285 m, the mountain where the Bible says the Ten Commandments were revealed to Moses

㉙ *Mount Kosciuszko, Oceania*—7,310 ft./2,228 m, highest mountain in Australia

㉚ *Mount Tai, Asia*—5,000 ft./1,524 m, one of the five holy mountains in China

㉛ *Ben Nevis, Scottish Highlands, Europe*—4,406 ft./1,343 m, highest mountain in Britain

㉜ *Mount Vesuvius, Europe*—4,203 ft./1,281 m

㉝ *Table Mountain, Cape Ranges, Africa*—3,563 ft./1,086 m

㉞ *Sugar Loaf, Southern Brazilian Highlands, South America*—1,296 ft./395 m

SMALLEST MOUNTAIN

㉟ *Mount Wycheproof, Oceania*—141 ft./43 m

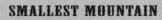

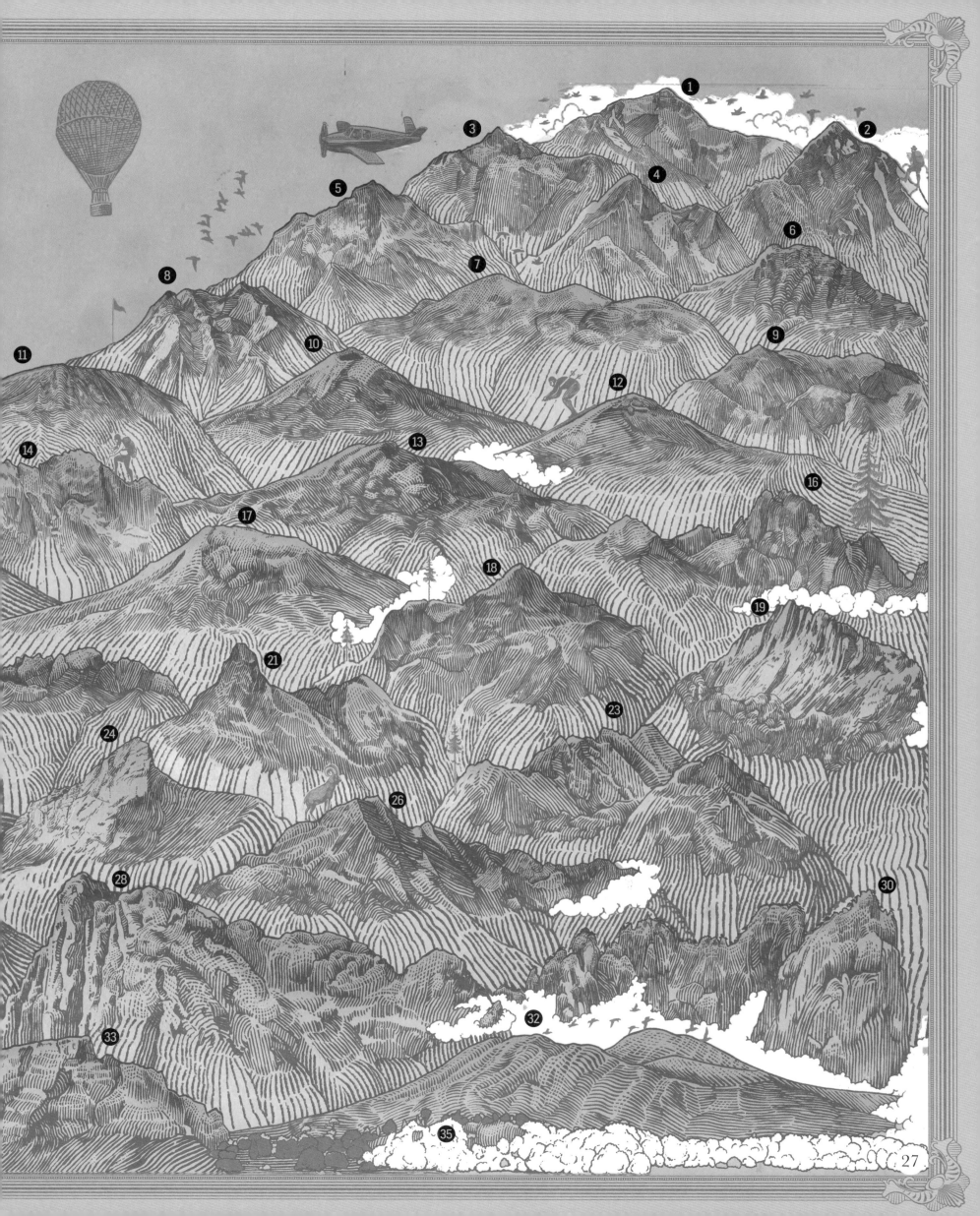

27

Deepest Oceans

SUNLIGHT ZONE

0 – 656 ft./ 0 – 200 m

Sunlight (euphotic) zone: there is enough sunlight for photosynthesis to take place. It is home to many creatures.

TWILIGHT ZONE

656 – 3,280 ft./ 200 – 1,000 m

Twilight (dysphotic) zone: sunlight decreases rapidly with depth, and photosynthesis is not possible. No plant life exists.

MIDNIGHT ZONE

3,280 ft./1,000 m+

Midnight (aphotic) zone: the pressure here is immense, there is no sunlight, and temperatures are near freezing.

At 13,100 ft./4,000 m, the abyssal zone begins. Here, rising from the ocean floor, colossal hydrothermal vents spew clouds of toxic fluids that are hot enough to melt lead.

AVERAGE DEPTHS OF THE WORLD'S OCEANS

ARCTIC OCEAN—3,953 ft./1,205 m

SOUTHERN OCEAN—10,728 ft./3,270 m

ATLANTIC OCEAN—11,962 ft./3,646 m

INDIAN OCEAN—12,274 ft./3,741 m

PACIFIC OCEAN—13,386 ft./4,080 m

The **Mariana Trench** is located near Guam in the Pacific Ocean and is where the deepest point of the world's oceans, Challenger Deep, is located.

On April 14, 1912, the huge ocean liner the *Titanic* hit an iceberg in the North Atlantic and sank with 1,500 people aboard. The wreck was finally discovered in 1985 at a depth of 12,467 ft./3,800 m.

Challenger Deep is deeper than the height of Mount Everest by more than a mile/ 2 km.

CHALLENGER DEEP

36,200 ft./ 11,034 m

Mount Everest is 29,029 ft. /8,848 m tall.

HMS *Challenger* explored the world's oceans, discovering many new species. In 1875, it also made the first recordings of the depths of the Mariana Trench.

In 2006, Chief Navy diver Daniel Jackson set a new record for a dive off the California coast of 2,000 ft./600 m. He wore an atmospheric diving system known as the Hardsuit 2000.

Scientists believe that around 80 percent of all volcanic eruptions on Earth occur in the ocean. The deepest eruption discovered so far is of the West Mata volcano, in an area between Samoa, Fiji, and Tonga, 3,950 ft./1,204 m beneath the surface of the Pacific Ocean.

The Perdido oil platform is the deepest floating oil rig. It lies under nearly 8,000 ft./2,450 m of ocean. In 2016, a different type of oil-production operation, called Stones, began retrieving oil from 9,500 ft./2,900 m down. Both Stones and Perdido are located in the Gulf of Mexico.

❶ **Tuna**
3–656 ft./1–200 m

❷ **Firefly squid**
1,200 ft./365 m

❸ **Barreleye fish**
2,600 ft./800 m

❹ **Vampire squid**
3,000 ft./900 m

❺ **Blobfish**
4,000 ft./1,200 m

❻ **Deep-sea anglerfish**
5,700 ft./1,750 m

❼ **Giant Pacific octopus**
6,600 ft./2,000 m

❽ **Giant tubeworms**
10,800 ft./3,300 m

❾ **Dumbo octopus**
13,100 ft./4,000 m

❿ **Pacific viperfish**
14,400 ft./4,390 m

⓫ Deepest known **hydrothermal vents** at a site called Beebe, Cayman Trough — 16,400 ft./5,000 m

⓬ **Snailfish**
26,700 ft./8,145 m

Burrowing Animals

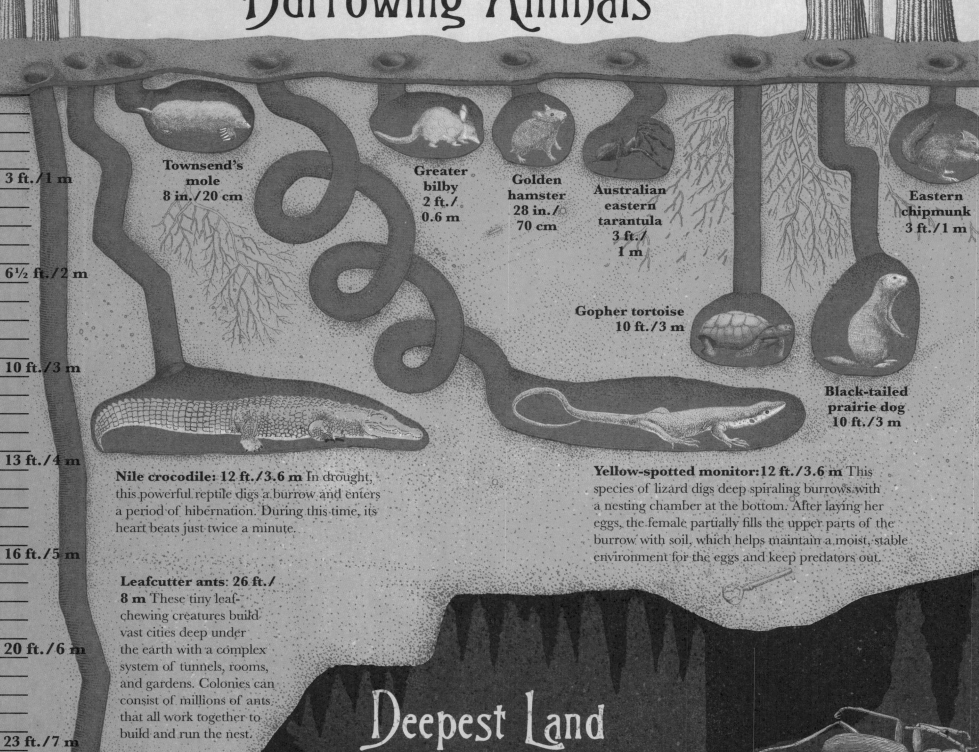

3 ft./1 m

6½ ft./2 m

10 ft./3 m

13 ft./4 m

16 ft./5 m

20 ft./6 m

23 ft./7 m

26 ft./8 m

30 ft./9 m

Townsend's mole
8 in./20 cm

Greater bilby
2 ft./0.6 m

Golden hamster
28 in./70 cm

Australian eastern tarantula
3 ft./1 m

Eastern chipmunk
3 ft./1 m

Gopher tortoise
10 ft./3 m

Black-tailed prairie dog
10 ft./3 m

Nile crocodile: 12 ft./3.6 m In drought, this powerful reptile digs a burrow and enters a period of hibernation. During this time, its heart beats just twice a minute.

Yellow-spotted monitor: 12 ft./3.6 m This species of lizard digs deep spiraling burrows with a nesting chamber at the bottom. After laying her eggs, the female partially fills the upper parts of the burrow with soil, which helps maintain a moist, stable environment for the eggs and keep predators out.

Leafcutter ants: 26 ft./ 8 m These tiny leaf-chewing creatures build vast cities deep under the earth with a complex system of tunnels, rooms, and gardens. Colonies can consist of millions of ants that all work together to build and run the nest.

Deepest Land Animals
3,215 ft./980 m+

4,590 ft./1,400 m
Duvalius abyssimus: a species of cave beetle recently discovered in the world's deepest cave, the Krubera, in southern Russia.

6,500 ft./1,980 m
Plutomurus ortobalaganensis: the world's deepest-living arthropod; wingless, eyeless, and only 3/16 in. long, it lives in total darkness in the Krubera Cave

All over the planet, animals make use of underground burrows to shelter from predators, keep warm, or store their food. Some species spend their whole lives underground; others hide there to give birth and raise their young.

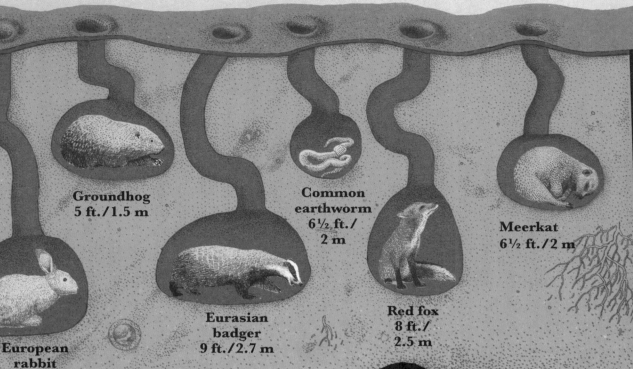

Groundhog
5 ft./1.5 m

Common earthworm
6½ ft./2 m

Meerkat
6½ ft./2 m

European rabbit
10 ft./3 m

Eurasian badger
9 ft./2.7 m

Red fox
8 ft./2.5 m

197 ft./60 m
People have been known to live underground too. A 5,000-year-old underground city in Derinkuyu, Turkey, was carved out of the rock and is thought to have housed up to 20,000 people. It contained stables, cellars, storage rooms, wineries, and even churches and schools.

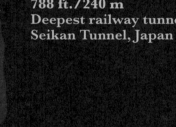

66 ft./20 m

130 ft./40 m

200 ft./60 m

260 ft./80 m

400 ft./120 m
Deepest tree roots

330 ft./100 m

656 ft./200 m

788 ft./240 m
Deepest railway tunnel, Seikan Tunnel, Japan

984 ft./300 m

1,312 ft./400 m

1,640 ft./500 m

2,000 ft./600 m

2,300 ft./700 m

2,600 ft./800 m

3,000 ft./900 m

3,280 ft./1,000 m

3,215 ft./980 m
Zospeum tholussum: a tiny, fragile snail found in Croatia's deepest cave system

3,810 ft./1,160 m
Little brown bats:
A colony of 1,000 individuals winter in a New York zinc mine at a record depth for any bat species.

9,843 ft./3,000 m

10,190 ft./3,106 m
Deepest single-shaft elevator in Moab Khotsong gold mine, South Africa

12,795 ft./3,900 m
The deepest point visited by human beings

11,800 ft./3,600 m
Unnamed species of **nematode:** the deepest-living animal ever found, in a gold mine in South Africa, where the temperatures are as high as 118°F/48°C

13,100 ft./4,000 m

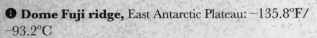

HOTTEST, COLDEST, DRIEST, WETTEST PLACES

Coldest Places on Earth

❶ **Dome Fuji ridge,** East Antarctic Plateau: −135.8°F/ −93.2°C
❷ **Dome Argus,** Antarctic Plateau: −135.4°F/−93°C
❸ **Vostok research station:** −128.6°F/−89.2°C
❹ **Scott South Pole Station:** −117°F/−82.8°C
❺ **Mount Denali,** Alaska: −100°F/−73.3°C
❻ **Klinck research station,** Greenland: −92.9°F/−69.4°C
❼ **Oymyakon,** Russia: −89.9°F/−67.7°C
❽ **Verkhoyansk,** Russia: −89.7°F/−67.6°C
❾ **North Ice,** Greenland: −87°F/−66°C
❿ **Snag,** Yukon, Canada: −81°F/−62.8°C

COLDEST PERMANENTLY INHABITED PLACE ON EARTH:
Grise Fiord, Nunavut, Canada has an average mean temperature of **2.3°F/−16.4°C.**

Hottest Places on Earth

❶ **Death Valley,** California: 129°F/ 54°C
❷ **Mitribah,** Kuwait: 129°F/54°C
❸ **Basra,** Iraq: 129°F/54°C
❹ **Mohenjo Daro,** Pakistan: 128°F/53.5°C
❺ **Lake Havasu City,** Arizona: 128°F/53.3°C
❻ **Turbat,** Pakistan: 127.4°F/53°C
❼ **Sibi,** Pakistan: 127.4°F/53°C
❽ **Dehloran,** Iran: 127.4°F/53°C
❾ **Gotvand,** Iran: 127.4°F/53°C
❿ **Nasiriyah,** Iraq: 127.4°F/53°C

HOTTEST PERMANENTLY INHABITED PLACE ON EARTH:
Mecca, Saudi Arabia, has an annual average temperature of **93.9°F/34.4°C.**

The Earth's crust makes up just 1 percent of the Earth's mass but is home to all known life in the universe.

A few of the world's largest modern volcanic eruptions

Volcanic eruptions are measured using the Volcanic Explosivity Index (VEI), which uses variables such as volume and rate to quantify a volcano's power; the scale goes from 1 to 8, and each VEI is ten times greater than the last.

Tambora, Indonesia, 1815 [VEI 7] The largest known modern eruption.
Krakatoa, Indonesia, 1883 [VEI 6] About 13,000 times more powerful than the atomic bomb that devastated Hiroshima
Mount Katmain, Alaska, 1912 [VEI 6] The largest terrestrial eruption of the twentieth century

Continental crust forms the land on which we live; it is older than oceanic crust and is 5–10 mi./8–16 km thick. Dynamic geological forces created Earth's crust, and the crust continues to be shaped by the planet's movement and energy.
The Mohorovicic discontinuity: the boundary between the crust and the mantle.

100 mi./ 160 km *Diamonds are formed.*

The Gutenberg discontinuity: the boundary between the mantle and the core.

The mantle has a depth of 6–1,800 mi./ 10–2,900 km. It is made of molten rock that flows under pressure, which causes earthquakes and volcanic eruptions. The mantle makes up 84% of the Earth's total volume.

The outer core has a depth of 1,800–3,200 mi./2,900–5,150 km. The liquid-iron outer core generates powerful magnetic fields that deflect cosmic rays from the sun, preventing them from reaching us at the surface.

The inner core has a depth of 3,200–4,000 mi./5,150– 6,400 km. The ball-shaped inner core is made mostly of iron and nickel. Although the core is extraordinarily hot, it stays solid because of the immense pressure surrounding it.

While you are unlikely to see giant serpents or three-headed hounds on your journey to the Earth's core, you may come across giant forests of crystals, reaching up to 6 mi./10 km high, and swirling lakes of molten metal. By the time you reach the very center, temperatures reach a scorching 10,800°F/6,000°C—which is about as hot as the sun.

The center of the Earth The pressure at the center of the Earth is extreme: 3.6 million atm—the same as if the Empire State Building were balanced on your head.

Supervolcanoes

The term supervolcano is used to describe a volcano that has had an eruption of more than 240 cubic miles/1,000 cubic kilometers of magma. Such events are very rare and usually hundreds of thousands of years apart but can have catastrophic effects on the planet.

❶ **Siberian Traps,** Siberia, Russia
250 million years ago
Erupted at the end of the Permian era and is thought to have wiped out 90 percent of life on Earth.

❷ **Wah Wah Springs,** Utah
30 million years ago [VEI 8]

❸ **Yellowstone,** Wyoming
640,000 years ago [VEI 8]

❹ **Toba,** Sumatra, Indonesia
74,000 years ago [VEI 8]
The Toba explosions released 672 cubic mi./ 2,800 cubic km of magma and left behind a huge depression, which is now a crater lake 62 mi./ 100 km long and 19 mi./30 km wide.

Driest Places on Earth

❶ **Arica,** Chile
Average annual rainfall: 0.761 mm
Located in the northern Atacama Desert, Arica holds the world record for the longest dry streak, having gone 173 months without a drop of rain in the early twentieth century. The dryness is so extreme that scientists study the soil in the surrounding Atacama Desert, as the conditions make the soil chemistry remarkably similar to that of Mars.

❷ **Al-Kufrah,** Libya
Average annual rainfall: 0.860 mm
The driest spot in Africa

❸ **Aswan,** Egypt
Average annual rainfall: 0.861 mm

❹ **Luxor,** Egypt
Average annual rainfall: 0.862 mm

❺ **Amundsen-Scott South Pole station,** Antarctica
Average annual rainfall: 2 mm

❻ **Ica,** Peru
Average annual rainfall: 2.29 mm

❼ **Wadi Halfa,** Sudan
Average annual rainfall: 2.45 mm

❽ **Iquique,** Chile
Average annual rainfall: 5.08 mm

❾ **Pelican Point,** Namibia
Average annual rainfall: 8.13 mm

❿ **Aoulef,** Algeria
Average annual rainfall: ½ in./12.19 mm

Wettest Places on Earth

❶ **Mawsynram,** Meghalaya, India
Average annual rainfall: 467 in./11,871 mm

❷ **Cherrapunji,** Meghalaya, India
Average annual rainfall: 464 in./11,777 mm

❸ **Mount Waialeale,** Kauai, Hawaii, N America
Average annual rainfall: 458 in./11,640 mm

❹ **Cropp River,** New Zealand
Average annual rainfall: 453 in./11,516 mm

❺ **San Antonio de Ureca,** Bioko Island, Equatorial Guinea
Average annual rainfall: 411 in./10,450 mm

❻ **Debundscha,** Cameroon
Average annual rainfall: 405 in./10,299 mm

❼ **Big Bog,** Maui, Hawaii, N America
Average annual rainfall: 404 in./10,272 mm

❽ **Puu Kukui,** Maui, Hawaii
Average annual rainfall: 366 in./9,293 mm

❾ **Quibdo,** Colombia, South America
Average annual rainfall: 354 in./8,990 mm

❿ **Mount Emei,** Sichuan Province, China
Average annual rainfall: 322 in./8,169 mm

UPPER MANTLE
2,552–5,432°F/
1,400–3,000°C

LOWER MANTLE
5,432°F/
3,000°C
pressure
40,000 atm

OUTER CORE
7,000–10,800°F/
4,000–6,000°C
pressure
1.35 million atm

INNER CORE
9,000–10,800°F/
4,000–6,000°C
pressure
3.25 million atm

CENTER OF THE EARTH pressure
3.6 million atm

What Lies Within
For many thousands of years, people from all cultures have imagined what lies deep beneath the Earth's crust.

In Hindu mythology, there are legends of a race called the Nagas. Half human, half serpent, these immortal creatures live in a subterranean kingdom called Naga-loka, or Patala-loka, where they guard great treasures.

To the ancient Greeks and Romans, it was Hades, an underworld of deep caverns, guarded by the fearsome three-headed dog Cerberus.

SOME OF THE WORLD'S
BIGGEST STORMS

❶ HURRICANES, TYPHOONS, and CYCLONES

Formed over warm waters, hurricanes, typhoons, and cyclones are among the most powerful and destructive weather systems on the planet. They bring with them two major perils — powerful winds and torrential rain — and can be devastating when they strike coastal areas. Hurricanes originate in the Atlantic and eastern Pacific, typhoons in the northwest Pacific, and cyclones in the Indian or South Pacific Oceans.

The Great Hurricane of 1780, Lesser Antilles, October 10–16, 1780
The deadliest Atlantic hurricane in history. More than 20,000 people were killed in the wake of this monster storm.

Cyclone Mahina, Bathurst Bay, March 4, 1899
This tropical cyclone produced the highest recorded storm surge, up to 43–48 ft./13–14.6 m. More than 300 people were killed after Mahina hit the Queensland, Australia, coastline, while fish and dolphins were reportedly found on top of 50-ft.-/15-m-high cliffs.

Super Typhoon Tip, northwest Pacific, October 4–24, 1979
This was the largest and most intense typhoon ever recorded, reaching a wind diameter of 1,380 mi./2,220 km — almost half the size of the United States. Its central pressure dropped to 26 inHg/870 hPa, the lowest sea-level pressure ever observed on Earth.

❷ ICE STORMS
Quebec Ice Storm, Canada, January 4–10, 1998
Producing more than 4 in./100 mm of freezing rain, this is often described as the twentieth century's worst ice storm.

❸ SNOWSTORMS
Storm of the Century, North America,
March 11–14, 1993
This epic storm unleashed snow and wind on a
wider area than any other in history. At its peak,
it stretched from Canada to Central America.
It left more than 270 dead. The Iran Blizzard of
1972 ranks as one of the deadliest snowstorms in
history, with around 4,000 killed.

❹ HAILSTORMS
Gopalganj, Bangladesh, April 14, 1986
The heaviest hailstones ever recorded, weighing
up to 2 lbs /1 kg and killing 92 people.

❺ SUPERCELLS and TORNADOES
2011 Super Outbreak, United States, April 25–28
The most extensive tornado outbreak on record
to date, resulting in 362 tornadoes and 321
fatalities.

❻ LIGHTNING
Catatumbo River, Venezuela
With 650 lightning flashes per square mile/
250 per square kilometer each year, Catatumbo
is reported to have the highest concentration of
lightning in the world. During the rainy season,
the area experiences an average of 28 lightning
flashes per minute.

COSMIC STORMS
These earthly storms are nothing compared
to those that occur in space. On Jupiter, a
tremendous storm known as the Great Red
Spot has been raging for 350 years and is
twice the size of Earth. Scientists meanwhile
have observed the so-called perfect cosmic
storm——two vast galaxy clusters colliding
together like high-pressure weather fronts to
create hurricane-like conditions and sending
100-million-degree gases spewing through
space.

PEREGRINE FALCON VS. GOLDEN EAGLE

GOLDEN EAGLE

This eagle dives at speeds of more than 150 mph/ 240 kmh, making it the second-fastest bird.

PEREGRINE FALCON

When making its high-speed stoop in pursuit of prey, the peregrine is the fastest bird on the planet.

Peregrine falcons can reach speeds of up to 120 mph/ 193 kmh and have been recorded plunge-diving for prey at up to 153 mph/ 250 kmh.

The Hum of a Hummingbird's Wing

ANNA'S HUMMINGBIRD

During its spectacular courtship dive, the exquisite male Anna's hummingbird zooms through the air like an iridescent fireball. As it reaches its top speed—an extraordinary 385 body lengths per second or 61 mph/98 kmh—it produces an explosive squeaking noise with its tail feathers.

The Supercharged Swift

In dramatic mating displays known as screaming parties, the aptly named swift can hit top speeds of 69 mph/ 111.6 kmh, flying horizontally and soaring upward.

THE COMMON SWIFT

A gray-headed albatross reached sustained speeds of 79 mph/ 127 kmh for nearly nine hours while returning to its nest at Bird Island, South Georgia, in the middle of an Antarctic storm.

GRAY-HEADED ALBATROSS

AUSTRALIAN DRAGONFLY— FASTEST INSECT IN THE AIR

Bugs

THE AERIAL BATTLES OF THE AUSTRALIAN DRAGONFLY

Taking the crown of the fastest insect on the planet is the Australian dragonfly. In an astonishing display of aerial acrobatics, these lethal hunters can hover, zigzag, and even fly backward at speeds of up to 36 mph/ 58 kmh.

SENSATIONAL SIX-LEGGED SPRINTERS

The Australian tiger beetle is the cheetah of the insect world, covering an incredible 5½ mph/9 kmh.

MIGHTY MINUSCULE MITE

The *Paratarsotomus macropalpis,* a mite from southern California no bigger than a sesame seed, was recorded traveling at an extraordinary 322 body lengths per second. That's equivalent to a human running at around 1,300 mph/2,000 kmh.

AUSTRALIAN TIGER BEETLE— FASTEST INSECT ON LAND

PARATARSOTOMUS MACROPALPIS

CHEETAH

FASTEST ANIMAL ON LAND

The secret to the fastest runner on Earth is its long, flexible spine, which means it can stretch out and flex its body as it runs at top speed, while its blunt claws provide powerful traction on the ground. It can accelerate from 0 to 55 mph/90 kmh in 3 seconds, which would leave most cars in the dust, and it can reach speeds of up to 60 mph/95 kmh. The cheetah can make quick and sudden turns in pursuit of prey, but it needs to strike fast. These chases cost the hunter a huge amount of energy and are usually over in less than a minute.

PRONGHORN

2ND-FASTEST ANIMAL ON LAND

Trailing just behind the speedy cheetah is the graceful pronghorn. When fleeing attack, it can hit speeds of around 53 mph/86 kmh. Other fast-footed land creatures include the springbok, the blackbuck, the blue wildebeest, Thomson's gazelle, and the brown hare.

FASTEST REPTILES

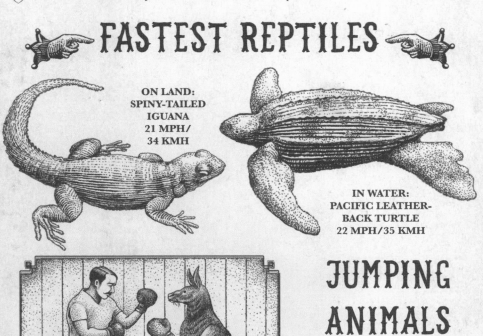

ON LAND: SPINY-TAILED IGUANA 21 MPH/ 34 KMH

IN WATER: PACIFIC LEATHER-BACK TURTLE 22 MPH/35 KMH

JUMPING ANIMALS

Red kangaroos are the world's fastest jumping mammals. They an travel at speeds of 35mph/ 56 kmh, covering 26 feet/ 8 meters in a single leap, and can jump 6 feet/1.8 meters high.

KANGAROO

Fastest Creatures in the Sea

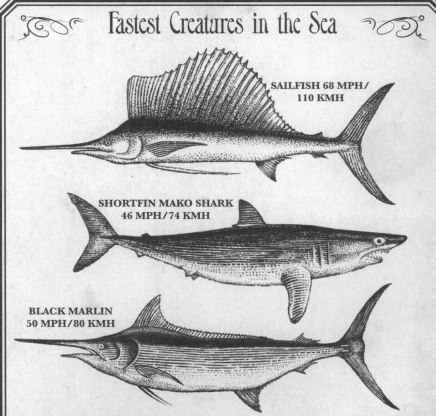

SAILFISH 68 MPH/ 110 KMH

SHORTFIN MAKO SHARK 46 MPH/74 KMH

BLACK MARLIN 50 MPH/80 KMH

Powerful and streamlined, the sailfish is considered the world's fastest fish — clocked leaping out of the water at speeds of more than 68 mph/ 110 kmh. It is closely followed by the marlin, while the mako is the speediest of the sharks.

Giant Forests under the Sea

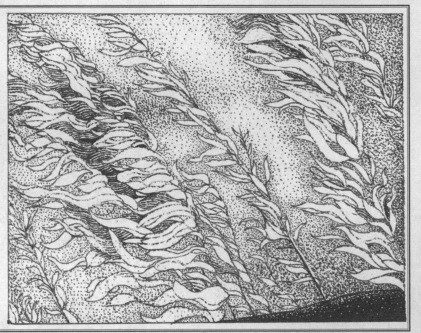

Stretching along the Californian coast, vast towers of giant kelp thrive in the sunshine. Anchored to the seabed by their "holdfasts," the kelp strands grow up toward the sunlight, forming a thick canopy on the surface of the water. They can grow by as much as 24 inches/60 centimeters a day, making them one of the fastest-growing organisms on Earth. Hundreds of creatures, from fish and sea urchins to sea otters and seals, seek shelter amid the kelp.

BAMBOO

The world record for the fastest-growing plant belongs to a certain species of bamboo, which can grow up to 35 inches/ 91 centimeters a day. Many animals, from mountain gorillas to giant pandas and spectacled bears, rely on bamboo for food, while bongos and bats take shelter between their woody stems.

37

LONGEST-LIVED ANIMALS

1001–3000 years

Black coral
More than 4,000 years

Black coral is the oldest marine organism living on Earth. Researchers collected some specimens found at depths of up to 1,600 feet/488 meters, and were able to determine its age in much the same way they do a tree, as these corals have growth rings showing how long they have lived.

351–1000 years

Ocean quahog
More than 500 years

The immortal jellyfish (*Turritopsis dohrnii*) is a jellyfish that can transform itself from an adult back into a baby, and can do it over and over again. Only as wide as a human fingernail when fully grown, the immortal jellyfish is capable of turning itself into a bloblike cyst, which then develops into a polyp colony, an early stage in a jellyfish's life. However, it does this only when threatened with starvation, physical damage, or other crises that would lead to certain death.

251–350 years

Giant tortoises are famously long-lived. The oldest recorded individual was a **radiated tortoise**, Tu'i Malila, of Tonga, who died at age 188. The **Galápagos tortoise** Harriet survived to around 176. Jonathan, a **Seychelles giant tortoise**, is currently the oldest living animal, at over 180 years old.

Aldabra giant tortoise
250 years
(anecdotal evidence)

Tube worms
250 years

151–250 years

Koi
228 years

A **koi** named Hanako is said to have reached the ripe old age of 228. Its age was estimated by counting the rings on its scales.

Bowhead whale
211 years

Bowhead whales live longer than any other mammal, in part due to their slow metabolism — an adaptation to the freezing oceanic waters of their Arctic habitat.

86–150 years

Greenland shark
150 years

Jeanne Calment
122 years (the world's oldest person whose age could be verified)

Tuatara
More than 100 years

Asian elephant
86 years

Muja, the world's oldest **alligator,** lives at the Belgrade Zoo, in Serbia. He has far exceeded the alligator life expectancy of about fifty years—and survived two bombing raids on the zoo during World War II that killed most of the zoo's inhabitants.

American alligator
More than 80 years

70–85 years

Laysan albatross
65 years

Brown bear
47 years

Greater flamingo
83 years

Major Mitchell's cockatoo
At least 83 years

Siberian white crane
82 years

British barge horse
62 years

Bornean orangutan
62 years

Old Billy, a working **barge horse,** was sixty-two years old when he died on November 27, 1822. He was born in Lancashire, England, and spent his life pulling barges along canals.

Japanese giant salamanders have the longest known life span of any amphibian.

55–69 years

Japanese giant salamander
55 years

Black rhino
50 years

Domestic cat
38 years

Polar bear
42 years

45–54 years

Rockhopper penguin
29 years

20–44 years

In the wild, **brown bears** have a life span of around twenty-five years. Cubs grow quickly, reaching 55 pounds/25 kilograms by six months. They continue to grow until they are eleven years old.

Some of the Shortest-Lived Animals

❶ The **mayfly** has the shortest adult life span of any insect—less than five minutes in one species. In its final winged stage, a mayfly's sole purpose is to mate, and in most species, death ensues shortly after.

❷ The adult **housefly** lives only between fifteen and twenty-five days. Some species can complete their entire life cycle in as little as seven days.

❸ A **dragonfly** spends up to two years in its larval form, beneath the water's surface. As adults, some last only two to three weeks.

❹ On average, a **house mouse** lives twelve to eighteen months, but it more than makes up for this reproductively, becoming sexually mature at five to seven weeks and having up to fourteen litters a year.

Most ABUNDANT Life-Forms

So far, scientists have cataloged 1.5 million species but haven't reached a consensus on the estimated total number of individual life-forms on Earth. Including species that are neither plants nor animals, such as lichens, mushrooms, and bacteria, the total number of life-forms could be as high as 30 million, but we really don't know yet.

BROWN RATS ❹ HUMANS ❽

❶ Bacteria
One estimate put the number of bacteria at 5 million trillion trillion, making them the most abundant life-form on Earth. The most numerous are thought to be members of the *Pelagibacterales*, which are estimated to make up 25 percent of the world's plankton.

❷ Viruses
The idea of viruses as life-forms is debatable: they cannot replicate on their own but can do so in host cells. They reproduce at a phenomenal rate.

❸ Bacteriophages
If viruses are classified as life-forms, then bacteriophages, the viruses that infect bacteria, are the most numerous of them all: a billion billion times more so than those that infect humans.

❹ Mammals
Humans, with a population count of more than 7 billion, are the most numerous mammals, closely followed by the **brown rat.**

❺ Birds
Red-billed queleas, whose population can reach as much as 10 billion, are the most abundant wild bird. The most numerous domestic bird is the **chicken,** at 24 billion.

❻ Reptiles
There are few studies quantifying the most numerous reptile species, but it is most likely to be a type of **lizard** or **snake.**

❼ Amphibians
Frogs and **toads** are estimated to be the most numerous amphibians, with more than 5,500 known species.

❽ Fish
Bristlemouths, or **lightfish** are considered the most numerous fish and the most common vertebrate on the planet, numbering in the hundreds of trillions.

❾ Crustaceans
In addition to being the world's most numerous crustacean, **copepods** may also be the world's most populous multi-celled organism.

❿ Arachnids
Ticks and mites are found in soil, water, and tall grasses, and are often parasites to other animals, including humans. The tiny mite outnumbers insects by ten to one.

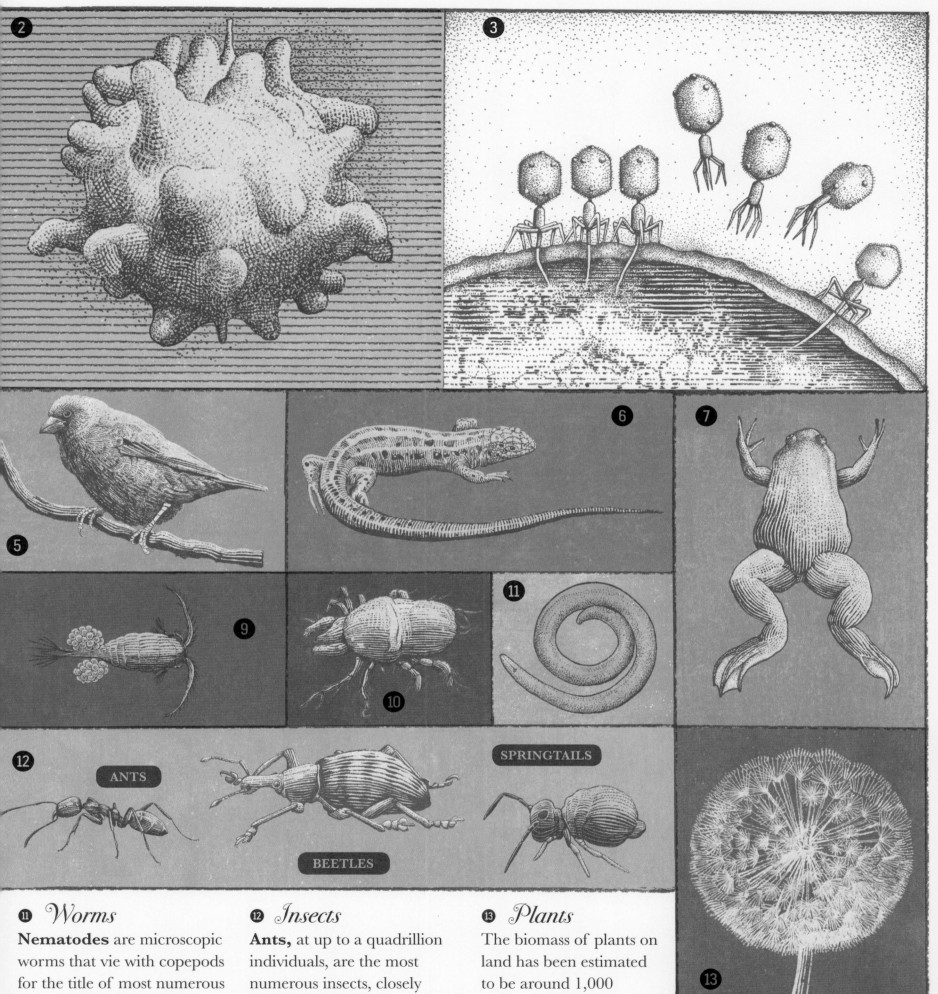

⑪ *Worms*

Nematodes are microscopic worms that vie with copepods for the title of most numerous multi-celled organism. A handful of soil contains thousands of them.

⑫ *Insects*

Ants, at up to a quadrillion individuals, are the most numerous insects, closely followed by **beetles**—about one in three insects alive today is a beetle. Relatives of insects called **springtails** are even more numerous: with 1,000 in a square foot/10,000 in a square meter of soil.

⑬ *Plants*

The biomass of plants on land has been estimated to be around 1,000 times that of animals. **Angiosperms,** or flowering plants, make up around 90 percent of all plant species.

Lost World OF Giants

Fossil discoveries have revealed an amazing world of extinct megafauna—enormous versions of creatures that live today. Imagine beavers the size of bears, sloths as large as elephants, and armadillos as big as cars. Many of these creatures lived alongside early humans and their cousins and may have either hunted them or been hunted by them. Most megafauna species died out due to dramatic climate changes around the end of the last Ice Age, 11,600 years ago.

CREATURES THEN

❶ *Hyracotherium* or *Eohippus*
Shoulder height: 12–24 in./30–60 cm
Weight: Up to 20 lbs./9 kg | Lived:
Europe, N. America, c. 55–33 mya
Not all prehistoric creatures were bigger than they are today. This early horse was around the size of a small dog.

**❷ *Mammuthus primigenius*
(woolly mammoth)**
Height: 10–11½ ft./3–3.5 m | Weight:
Up to 7 tons/6.6 metric tons | Lived:
Asia, Europe, N. America, c. 700,000–4,000 ya | The woolly mammoth was similar in size to the average elephant. Unlike its modern

relative, it had a coat of thick, curly fur to keep it warm in the cold temperatures and curved tusks that could grow more than 13 feet/4 meters long. It was once thought that the mummified remains of mammoths discovered in the Siberian permafrost belonged to giant burrowing animals that died as soon as they were exposed to sunlight.

❸ *Titanoboa cerrejonensis*
Length: 43–48 ft./13–14.6 m | Weight:
2,500 lbs./1 metric ton | Lived:
S. America, c. 60–58 mya | This monstrous snake lived in the rain forests of South America millions of years ago. It was longer than a bus and capable of swallowing a crocodile whole.

❹ *Paraceratherium* or *Indricotherium*
Shoulder height: Up to 18 ft./5.5 m
(up to 26 ft./8 m with its head raised)
Weight: 16½–22 tons/15–20 metric tons
Lived: Europe and Asia, c. 30–16.6 mya
This enormous plant-eating rhinoceros was perhaps the largest land mammal of all time. With its head raised, it stood twice as tall as an elephant. It used its long, thick neck to reach leaves high in the treetops.

❺ *Castoroides*
Length: Up to 8 ft./2.5 m | Weight: Up to 275 lbs./125 kg | Lived: N. America, c. 1.4 mya–10,000 ya | These bear-size beavers had cutting teeth that could grow up to 6 inches/15 centimeters long.

❻ *Megalania prisca*
Length: Up to 18 ft./5.5 m | Weight: Up to 1,300 lbs./600 kg | Lived: Australia, c. 1.8 mya–40,000 ya | Fossil finds suggest that this terrifying ancient lizard feasted on Komodo dragons and giant kangaroos. It is thought that in addition to its very sharp teeth it also had toxic saliva that sent its victims into shock.

❼ *Glyptodon clavipes*
Length: Up to 11 ft./3.3 m | Weight:
Up to 4,400 lbs./2 metric tons | Lived:
S. and N. America, c. 5.3 mya–11,700 ya
This huge armadillo was roughly the size and shape of a Volkswagen Beetle. It was armed with a thick, rigid shell and a powerful spiked tail that it could swing like a baseball bat. To get past

the *Glyptodon*'s armor to its soft belly, predators would have needed to flip it over onto its back–no easy task given its bulk!

8 *Megatherium americanum*
Length: Up to 20 ft./6 m | Weight: Up to 4 tons/3.8 metric tons | Lived: S. America, c. 1.8 mya–10,000 ya
This mega-size sloth usually walked on all fours, but its fossilized footprints show that it could also walk on two legs for short distances, leaving its arms and claws free to grab twigs and leaves. When standing upright, it would have been as tall as a two-story house.

CREATURES NOW

A *Equus ferus caballus* (horse)
Shoulder height: Up to 5½ ft./1.7 m
Weight: Up to 2,000 lbs./900 kg
Lives: Worldwide, except polar regions

B *Loxodonta africana*
(African elephant)
Height: Up to 13 ft./4m | Weight: Up to 7 tons/6.3 metric tons | Lives: Africa
Elephants are the biggest and heaviest land creatures alive today.

C *Boa constrictor*
(boa constrictor)
Length: Up to 13 ft./4 m | Weight: Up to 60 lbs./27 kg | Lives: Central and S. America

D *Rhinocerotidae*
(white rhinoceros)
Shoulder height: Up to 6½ ft./2 m
Weight: Up to 4 tons/3.6 metric tons
Lives: Africa, Asia

E *Castor canadensis*
(American beaver)
Length (not including tail): Up to 35½ in./90 cm | Weight: Up to 70 lbs./32 kg | Lives: N. America

F *Varanus niloticus*
(Nile monitor lizard)
Length: Up to 8 ft./2.4 m | Weight: Up to 33 lbs./15 kg | Lives: Africa

G *Priodontes maximus*
(Giant armadillo)
Length (not including tail): Up to

3 ft./1 m | Weight: Up to 70 lbs./32 kg
Lives: S. America

H *Choloepus hoffmanni*
(Hoffman's two-toed sloth)
Length: Up to 30 in./75 cm | Weight: Up to 20 lbs./9 kg | Lives: Central and S. America

ya = years ago
Megafauna–The term *megafauna* is used to describe large (*mega*) animals (*fauna*) with an adult body weighes more than 99 pounds/45 kilograms. Humans are actually megafauna, as are elephants, giraffes, whales, and lions.

43

Birds Today

Ⓐ *Diomedea exulans* (**wandering albatross**)
Wingspan: Up to 11½ ft./3.5 m | Lives: Southern Hemisphere | Has the longest wingspan of any living bird

Ⓑ *Vultur gryphus* (**Andean condor**)
Wingspan: Up to 10½ ft./3.2 m | Lives: S. America

Ⓒ *Aquila chrysaetos* (**golden eagle**)
Wingspan: Up to 7½ ft./2.3 m Lives: Africa, Asia, Central and N. America, Europe

Ⓓ *Pica pica* (**common magpie**)
Wingspan: Up to 22 in./57 cm | Lives: Africa, Asia, Europe

Ⓔ *Apteryx* (**kiwi**)
Length: Up to 18 in./45 cm | Lives: New Zealand
The closest living relative of the elephant bird

Ⓕ *Struthio camelus* (**common ostrich**)
Height: Up to 9 ft./2.8 m | Lives: Africa
The largest bird alive today

Ⓖ *Caloenas nicobarica* (**Nicobar pigeon**)
Length: Up to 16 in./40 cm | Lives: S.E. Asia and the Pacific | The dodo's closest living relative

BIRDS & PTEROSAURS

During the time of the dinosaurs, the skies were ruled by flying reptiles known as pterosaurs. Some were small enough to fit in the palm of a hand, but one of the largest — the *Quetzalcoatlus* — was as tall as a giraffe and had the wingspan of a small airplane. The pterosaurs died out around 66 million years ago, making way for another group of flying animals: birds. Over millions of years, birds have evolved into an array of shapes, colors, and sizes, but none have ever reached the enormous size of the biggest pterosaurs.

Flying Creatures Then

❶ *Quetzalcoatlus northropi*
Wingspan: 33–36 ft./10–11 m | Lived: America, c. 68–66 mya | When the fossilized remains of this giraffe-size pterosaur were found in the American desert, people marveled that creatures that large could fly. Its secret lay in its hollow arm bones, which made it very lightweight. It also kept its wing beats to a minimum and used its wings of toughened skin to glide great distances. It was probably a scavenger and used its long neck to reach into the carcasses of dinosaurs.

❷ *Pelagornis sandersi*
Wingspan: 20–24 ft./6.1–7.4 m | Lived: N. America, c. 28–25 mya | This enormous seabird glided over ancient oceans millions of years ago. With a wingspan longer than a stretch limousine, it competes with the *Argentavis magnificens* for the title of largest flying bird of all time.

❸ *Argentavis magnificens*
Wingspan: 21–25 ft./6.5–7.5 m | Lived: S. America, c. 6 mya | This huge bird is an ancestor of the giant condor.

❹ *Archaeopteryx lithographica* — "The first bird"
Height: 12 in./30 cm | Lived: Europe, c. 150 mya
Birds evolved not from pterosaurs but from small, meat-eating dinosaurs. The magpie-size *Archaeopteryx* is often thought of as the missing link between dinosaurs and birds. It was a primitive bird with feathers, but unlike modern birds, it had a long tail and a full set of teeth. It is likely that it could fly at least short distances.

❺ *Harpagornis moorei* (Haast's eagle)
Wingspan: Up to 10 ft./3 m | Lived: New Zealand, c. 1.8 mya–1400 CE | One of the largest eagles that ever existed.

Flightless Birds Then

❻ *Dinornis robustus* (giant moa)
Height: Up to 12 ft./ 3.6 m | Lived: New Zealand, c. 8.5 mya–1450 CE | The giant moa was one of the biggest flightless birds ever to have lived. It had large legs but no wings and was hunted to extinction by Maori settlers, who ate its meat and used its skin, feathers, and bones to make clothes, fish hooks, and pendants.

❼ *Aepyornis maximus* (elephant bird)
Height: Up to 10 ft./3 m | Lived: Madagascar, c. 2 mya–1650 CE | Hundreds of years ago, adventurer Marco Polo came back from his travels with stories of a bird so big that it could swoop down, snatch an elephant in its talons, and fly through the air with it. In truth, the "elephant bird" was a flightless herbivore.

❽ *Titanis walleri*
Height: 8–10 ft./2.5–3 m | Lived: N. America, c. 4.9–1.8 mya | One of the last of the "terror birds," the *Titanis* was one of the top predators of its day. One theory is that it pinned prey to the ground with its claws, then swung its massive hooked beak at the creature like a pickax.

❾ *Raphus cucullatus* (dodo)
Height: Up to 3 ft./1 m | Lived: Mauritius, until c. 1662 CE | These clumsy flightless birds lived and nested on the ground. They were discovered in the 1500s by Dutch explorers, and only a hundred years later, they were extinct. Many had been eaten by the settlers, while their eggs had been eaten by pigs, cats, and other animals that had been introduced to the island.

Sea Creatures Then AND Now

For hundreds of years, people have told tales of colossal sea creatures that could tear apart ships and drag sailors to a watery grave. Step back in time millions of years, and the oceans were home to real live monsters — fearsome predatory whales, giant crocodiles, and megatoothed sharks that were three times the size of a great white shark. The largest animal ever to have lived — the blue whale — still lives in our oceans today. Despite its size, it is harmless to humans and lives on a diet of tiny crustaceans.

SEA CREATURES THEN

❶ Livyatan melvillei

Length: Up to 59 ft./18 m | Lived: S. America, c. 13–12 mya | Named after the biblical sea monster and Herman Melville, the author of *Moby-Dick*, this predatory whale had gigantic teeth more than 14 in./36 cm long. It is thought that it patrolled the world's oceans, feasting on baleen whales.

❷ Basilosaurus isis (genus name means "king lizard")

Length: Up to 59 ft./18 m | Lived: N. Africa, N. America, Asia, c. 40–30 mya | Despite their name, these fearsome predators were not reptiles. They were enormous ancient whales. They had long, snakelike bodies and a powerful bite capable of crunching through bones. There is evidence that, like modern killer whales, they even preyed on other whales.

❸ Carcharocles megalodon (species name means "megatooth")

Length: Up to 59 ft./18 m | Lived: Oceans around the world, c. 23–2.6 mya | These colossal sharks were around three times longer than a great white, and their jaws were 9 ft./2.7 m tall — big enough to swallow a human whole. A single *megalodon* tooth was more than 6 in./15 cm long and was used to tear into the flesh and crush the bones of other sea animals. Many years ago, fossilized shark teeth found washed up on the shore were thought to be the petrified tongues of dragons or snakes.

❹ Shonisaurus sikanniensis sp. nov. (genus name means "lizard from the Shoshone Mountains")

Length: Up to 69 ft./21 m | Lived: N. America, c. 220 mya | One of the largest marine reptiles that has yet been found, the *Shonisaurus* was longer than most modern whales. It had a short, toothless snout and is thought to have been a filter feeder, sucking in food through its open jaws.

❺ Machimosaurus Rex (means "fighting lizard king")

Length: Up to 33 ft./10 m | Lived: N. Africa, c. 132–129 mya | This ancient crocodile ancestor was as long as a bus, and its skull alone was as long as a person is tall. Its massive jaws were filled with sharp bullet-shaped teeth that it used to crunch through the shells of turtles.

SEA CREATURES NOW

Ⓐ Balaenoptera musculus (blue whale)

Length: Up to 105 ft./32 m | Lives: All oceans except enclosed seas and the Arctic Bigger than any dinosaur, the blue whale is as long as a Boeing 737 airplane.

Ⓑ Carcharodon carcharias (great white shark)

Length: Up to 20 ft./6 m | Lives: Oceans around the world

Ⓒ Crocodylus porosus (saltwater crocodile)

Length: Up to 18 ft./5.5 m | Lives: Indian and Pacific Oceans

Land of the Dinosaurs

For more than 160 million years, dinosaurs dominated our planet. They came in many different forms—from giant, peaceful plant eaters to sturdy armored stegosaurs and carnivorous theropods. Many of them would have towered over even the biggest creatures alive today. Others, like the chicken-size *Compsognathus*, were surprisingly small.

DINOSAURS CAN BE GROUPED INTO
THREE MAIN TYPES:

Theropods— *mostly meat eaters with powerful legs and short arms*
Ornithischians— *bird-hipped, herbivorous, and often armored dinosaurs*
Sauropods— *herbivores with long necks and tails; walked on four feet*

Tyrannosaurus rex
A fierce hunter and scavenger, and one of the most famous of the theropods
TYPE: **Theropod**
LENGTH: Up to 40 ft./12.3 m
HEIGHT: Up to 16 ft./5 m

Triceratops horridus—A four-legged dinosaur with three horns, a horny beak, and a bony frill
TYPE: **Ornithischian**
LENGTH: 26–30 ft./8–9 m
HEIGHT: Up to 10 ft./3 m (to top of head)

Stegosaurus stenops—The most famous of the stegosaurs, a group of slow-moving, plant-eating dinosaurs with bony plates or spikes on their backs
TYPE: **Ornithischian**
LENGTH: Up to 30 ft./9 m
HEIGHT: Up to 11½ ft./3.5 m
PLATES: Up to 24 in./60 cm wide and tall

Iguanodon bernissartensis
An example of an ornithopod dinosaur, which walked and ran on two back feet
TYPE: **Ornithischian**
LENGTH: 33–43 ft./10–13 m
HEIGHT: Up to 11 ft./3.3 m

Sauroposeidon proteles
Thought to be the tallest dinosaur ever to have walked the Earth, this massive herbivore was bigger than a six-story building and had legs as thick as tree trunks. Despite its overall size, its head was around the same size as that of a horse.
TYPE: **Sauropod**
LENGTH: 112 ft./34 m
HEIGHT: 59 ft./18 m

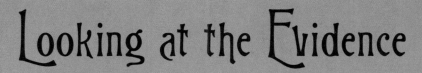

Looking at the Evidence

GIANT BONES

Measuring as much as 8 ft./2.4 m, the thighbone of the monster-size *Titanosaurus* is bigger than an adult human.

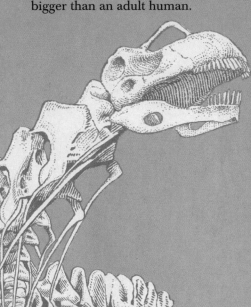

DINOSAUR TEETH

Dinosaur teeth hold many clues about what and how these creatures ate. The meat-eating *Tyrannosaurus* had teeth as long as bread knives, and its bite was at least three times as powerful as that of a lion. The plant-eating *Triceratops*, on the other hand, may have had as many as eight hundred teeth, stacked in columns, although only a small number of these were in use at any one time.

1. *Spinosaurus*
Up to 9 in./22.5 cm
Long and spearlike, for catching fish

2. *Tyrannosaurus*
Up to 8 in./20 cm
Had serrated edges used for tearing flesh and crunching bones

3. *Diplodocus*
Up to 3 in./8 cm
Narrow and peglike, used for stripping leaves from trees and raking through vegetation

4. *Triceratops*
Up to 2 in./5 cm
Used for shearing vegetation

5. Lion
Up to 4 in./ 10 cm

6. Human
Up to ½ in./ 1.25 cm

MONSTER EGGS

The smallest dinosaur eggs were the size of tennis balls; the biggest were like giant soccer balls. Compared with their enormous size, the mighty sauropods laid surprisingly small eggs — in fact, not much larger than an ostrich's egg. Scientists think that these smaller eggs may have taken less time to hatch and so reduced the risk of their being eaten by predators.

1. Chicken egg — 2¼ in./5.7 cm

2. Ostrich egg — 6 in./15 cm

3. *Titanosaurus* (sauropod) egg — 8½ in./ 22 cm

How Big?

See how these different giants measured up.

66 ft./20 m
59 ft./18 m
52 ft./16 m
46 ft./14 m
39 ft./12 m
33 ft./10 m
26 ft./8 m
20 ft./6 m
13 ft./4 m

Triceratops *Iguanodon* *Stegosaurus* *Diplodocus* Giraffe *Tyrannosaurus* Human *Spinosaurus* *Sauroposeidon*

TALL STRUCTURES *Then & Now*

Dinosaurs may have been the tallest creatures ever to have roamed the Earth, but they look mouselike when compared with some of the great buildings of the world. Throughout history, humans have built some extraordinary structures—from the mysterious columns of Stonehenge to the white marble domes of the Taj Mahal. Dwarfing them all for around 3,800 years was the Great Pyramid of Giza—a glittering monument to the mighty ancient Egyptian civilization.

❶ **33 ft./10 m**—Stonehenge, Wiltshire, England, c. 3000–2500 BCE

❷ **39 ft./12 m**—Statue of Zeus, Olympia, Greece, c. 430 BCE *

❸ **59 ft./18 m**—Temple of Artemis, Ephesus, Turkey, c. 550 BCE; rebuilt c. 356 BCE *

❹ **69 ft./21 m**—Cleopatra's Needle, Heliopolis, Egypt, c. 1460 BCE, now located in London, England

❺ **79 ft./24 m**—El Castillo, Chichén Itzá, Mexico, c. 1000–1200 CE

❻ **105 ft./32 m**—Colossus of Rhodes, Rhodes, Greece, c.294–282 BCE *

❼ **125 ft./38 m**—Christ the Redeemer statue, Rio de Janeiro, Brazil, 1931 (height includes the pedestal)

❽ **157 ft./48 m**—Colosseum, Rome, Italy, 80 CE

❾ **164 ft./50 m**—Arc de Triomphe, Paris, France, 1836

❿ **183 ft./55.7 m**—Leaning Tower of Pisa, Pisa, Italy, 1360

⓫ **187 ft./57 m**—Saint Basil's Cathedral, Moscow, Russia, 1554–1560

⓬ **197 ft./60 m**—Big Wild Goose Pagoda, Shaanxi province, China, 652

⓭ **239 ft./73 m**—Taj Mahal, Agra, India, 1653

⓮ **305 ft./93 m**—Statue of Liberty, New York, US, 1886 (height includes the pedestal)

⓯ **361 ft./110 m**—Lighthouse of Alexandria, Egypt, c. 280 BCE (the tallest lighthouse ever built) *

⓰ **364 ft./111.3 m**—Saint Paul's Cathedral, London, England, 1711

⓱ **435 ft./132.5 m**—Saint Peter's Basilica, Rome, Italy, 1626

⓲ **453 ft./138.8 m**—Great Pyramid of Giza, Cairo, Egypt, c.2580–2560 BCE (the only surviving Wonder of the Ancient World, and the tallest human-made structure in the world for about 3,800 years; when built, it stood 481 ft./146.5 m tall) *

⓳ **555 ft./169.1 m**—Washington Monument, Washington, D.C., 1884 (the world's tallest structure from 1884 to 1889)

* Wonder of the Ancient World

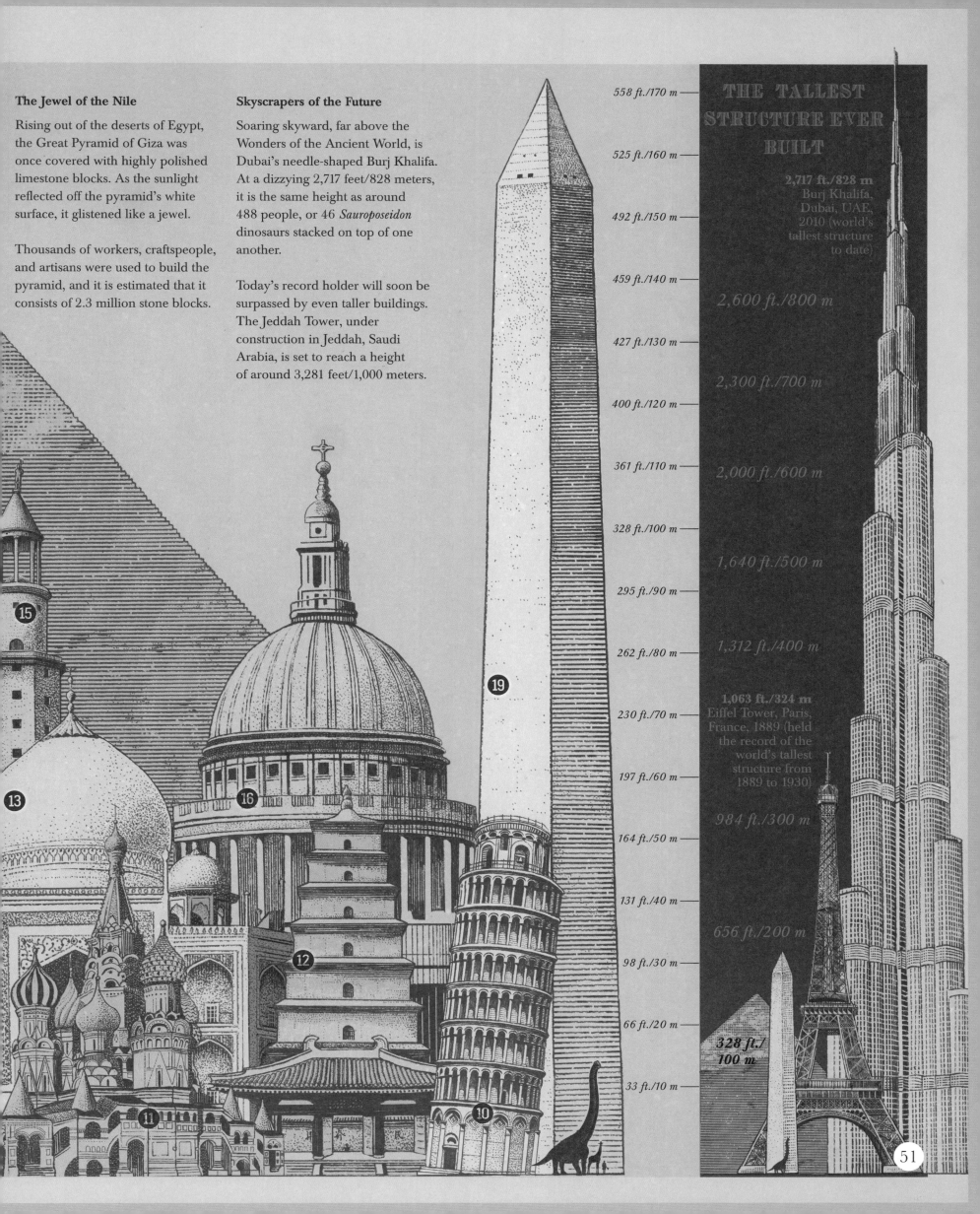

The Jewel of the Nile

Rising out of the deserts of Egypt, the Great Pyramid of Giza was once covered with highly polished limestone blocks. As the sunlight reflected off the pyramid's white surface, it glistened like a jewel.

Thousands of workers, craftspeople, and artisans were used to build the pyramid, and it is estimated that it consists of 2.3 million stone blocks.

Skyscrapers of the Future

Soaring skyward, far above the Wonders of the Ancient World, is Dubai's needle-shaped Burj Khalifa. At a dizzying 2,717 feet/828 meters, it is the same height as around 488 people, or 46 *Sauroposeidon* dinosaurs stacked on top of one another.

Today's record holder will soon be surpassed by even taller buildings. The Jeddah Tower, under construction in Jeddah, Saudi Arabia, is set to reach a height of around 3,281 feet/1,000 meters.

558 ft./170 m

525 ft./160 m

492 ft./150 m

459 ft./140 m

427 ft./130 m

400 ft./120 m

361 ft./110 m

328 ft./100 m

295 ft./90 m

262 ft./80 m

230 ft./70 m

197 ft./60 m

164 ft./50 m

131 ft./40 m

98 ft./30 m

66 ft./20 m

33 ft./10 m

THE TALLEST STRUCTURE EVER BUILT

2,717 ft./828 m
Burj Khalifa, Dubai, UAE, 2010 (world's tallest structure to date)

2,600 ft./800 m

2,300 ft./700 m

2,000 ft./600 m

1,640 ft./500 m

1,312 ft./400 m

1,063 ft./324 m
Eiffel Tower, Paris, France, 1889 (held the record of the world's tallest structure from 1889 to 1930)

984 ft./300 m

656 ft./200 m

328 ft./ 100 m

Towers, Waterfalls, AND Mountains

3,280 ft./1,000 m
Jeddah Tower, Jeddah, Saudi Arabia (under construction)

3,280 ft./
1,000 m

3,000 ft./
900 m

2,625 ft./
800 m

2,297 ft./
700 m

1,968 ft./
600 m

1,640 ft./
500 m

1,312 ft./
400 m

984 ft./
300 m

656 ft./
200 m

328 ft./
100 m

52

Towers AND Waterfalls

Peeking through the clouds, hundreds of feet above the streets below, skyscrapers dominate the skylines of cities around the world. Rising higher still is the magnificent Angel Falls. Hidden deep in the jungle of Venezuela, shrouded in mist, this spectacular waterfall is one of the greatest natural wonders on Earth.

Towers
❶ 2,717 ft./828 m—Burj Khalifa, Dubai, UAE, 2010
The world's current tallest structure
❷ 2,073 ft./632 m—Shanghai Tower, Shanghai, China, 2015
❸ 1,972 ft./601 m—Makkah Royal Clock Tower, Mecca, Saudi Arabia, 2012
❹ 1,775 ft./541 m—One World Trade Center, New York, 2014
❺ 1,667 ft./508 m—Taipei 101, Taipei, Taiwan, 2004

Waterfall
❻ 3,212 ft./979 m—Angel Falls, Bolívar State, Venezuela
The world's highest uninterrupted waterfall

Rivers of Gold and Devil Spirits
In 1937, the aviator and adventurer Jimmie Angel crash-landed his four-seater plane on a mountaintop. He was searching for a legendary river of gold, but what he came upon instead was a half-mile-high waterfall that would come to be named for him, Angel Falls. The falls were already well known to the local Pemon people as Kerepakupai-Merú, or "waterfall of the deepest place." The Pemon believed that it was home to devil spirits called *mawari,* who stole the souls of the living.

Mountains

The world's tallest towers and waterfalls pale in comparison with the largest mountains. Mount Everest is the same height as more than ten Burj Khalifas stacked on top of one another. Yet even the mighty Himalayas look tiny compared with the highest mountain in our solar system: Olympus Mons.

Highest Waterfall
❼ 3,212 ft./979 m—Angel Falls

Highest Mountains by Continent
❽ 16,024 ft./4,884 m—Mount Puncak Jaya or Carstensz Pyramid, *highest peak in Oceania*

❾ 16,066 ft./4,897 m—Mount Vinson, *highest peak in Antarctica*

❿ 18,510 ft./5,642 m—Mount Elbrus, *highest peak in Europe*

⓫ 19,340 ft./5,895 m—Mount Kilimanjaro, *highest peak in Africa*

⓬ 20,308 ft./6,191 m—Mount Denali, *highest peak in N. America*

⓭ 22,841 ft./6,962 m—Mount Aconcagua, *highest peak in S. America*

⓮ 29,029 ft./8,848 m— Mount Everest, *highest peak in Asia and highest mountain peak on Earth from sea level*

⓯ 33,481 ft./10,205 m— Mauna Kea, Hawaii, N. America, *tallest mountain peak on Earth measured from its base*

Although Mount Everest is the highest mountain on Earth measured from sea level, the tallest when measured from its base is Mauna Kea. The peak of this volcano rises 13,796 feet/ 4,205 meters from sea level, but its base plunges a further 19,685 feet/6,000 meters deep under the sea.

Highest Mountain in the Solar System
⓰ 15½ mi./25 km Olympus Mons, Mars

Olympus Mons, on the planet Mars, is almost three times taller than Mount Everest and covers an area the size of Arizona.

6.8 mi./ 11 km—Commercial aircraft cruising altitude height

7 mi./11.2 km – Rüppell's griffon vulture

15½ mi./ 25 km

12 mi./ 20 km

9 mi./ 15 km

6 mi./ 10 km

3 mi./ 5 km

2½ mi/ 4 km

2 mi/ 3 km

1½ mi/ 2 km

½ mi./ 1 km

SHIPS, TRAINS, AND TRUCKS

Ships, trains, and trucks are used around the globe to transport people and haul all kinds of things, from iron ore, food, and coal to cars, tanks, aircraft parts, and even garbage. They have allowed people to travel farther and carry heavier loads than ever before, to explore new worlds, and to discover treasures from distant lands.

SHIPS

SANTA MARIA
(1460–1492)
TYPE: Carrack **COUNTRY:** Spain
LENGTH: Estimated 98 ft./30 m

Person in a canoe

The *Santa Maria* was the biggest of Christopher Columbus's three ships on his 1492 voyage. It was designed to carry lots of cargo, and there were more than forty people on board — including a carpenter, a painter, a goldsmith, a tailor, and four known criminals.

CUTTY SARK
(1869–present)
TYPE: Clipper **COUNTRY:** UK
LENGTH: 213 ft./64.8 m

Person in a canoe

Built to transport tea from China to London, this famous cargo ship could carry as many as 10,000 tea chests — enough for 200 million cups. As well as tea, it carried everything from coffee, coal, cocoa beans and beer to wool, whale oil, shark bones, sardines, and straw hats.

RMS *TITANIC*
Santa Maria
(1911–1912)
TYPE: Ocean liner **COUNTRY:** UK
LENGTH: 883 ft./269 m

This famous steamship was the biggest and most luxurious ocean liner of its day. Stood on its end, it would have been the same height as three Statues of Liberty stacked on top of one another and almost as tall as the Eiffel Tower.

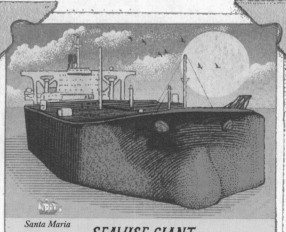

SEAWISE GIANT
Santa Maria
(1979–2010)
TYPE: Crude-oil tanker **COUNTRY:** Japan
LENGTH: 1,503 ft./458 m

This supertanker was the longest sea vessel ever built. Stood on its end, it would have been taller than the Empire State Building, and its holds were big enough to contain four Saint Paul's Cathedrals.

BHP IRON ORE TRAIN
(2001)
TYPE: Freight train
COUNTRY: Australia
LENGTH: 24,124 ft./7,353 m

Freight trains are some of the longest vehicles in the world. They use less fuel than trucks and are able to carry bigger loads over long distances. The biggest freight train of them all—the BHP iron ore train—was driven by eight locomotives and pulled 680 wagons across the Australian desert.

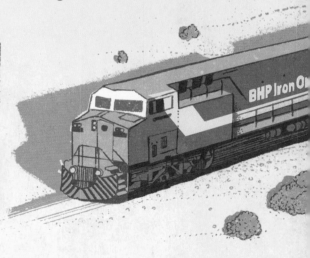

UNION PACIFIC "BIG BOY"
(1941–1962)
TYPE: Steam locomotive
COUNTRY: USA
LENGTH: 133 ft./40.47 m (including the tender)

This steam locomotive was one of the largest ever built. In its heyday, it pulled heavy freight trains over the mountains of Wyoming and Utah.

UNION PACIFIC

TRAINS

PENYDARREN LOCOMOTIVE
(1804)
TYPE: Steam locomotive
COUNTRY: UK
LENGTH: 25 ft./7.57 m (including the tender)
On February 21, 1804, Richard Trevithick's Penydarren locomotive hauled five wagons loaded with 11 tons/10 metric tons of iron ore and seventy people. It was the world's first steam locomotive journey on rails.

TRUCKS

BIGFOOT 5
(1986–present)
TYPE: Monster truck **COUNTRY:** USA
LENGTH: Around 21 ft./6.5 m long, 15 ft./4.7 m tall
Bigfoot 5 is the largest monster truck of all time. Its tires alone stand 10 feet/3 meters tall. The hefty tires once belonged to the Sno-Train, a U.S. military vehicle that took supplies over deep snow to remote Arctic locations.

BELAZ 75710 MINING DUMP TRUCK
(2014–present)
TYPE: Haul truck **COUNTRY:** Belarus
LENGTH: 68 ft./20.6 m
The world's biggest mining truck hauls loads of metal ore weighing more than 44 tons/40 metric tons. Temperatures in the mines can range from -58°F/-50°C to +122°F/+50°C.

AUSTRALIAN ROAD TRAIN
(2013–present)
TYPE: Heavy truck **COUNTRY:** Australia
LENGTH: 174 ft./53 m
Australian "power trains" are some of the world's longest trucks. They are used to carry such heavy goods as machinery, fuel, cattle, and gold for thousands of miles across the Australian desert.

Great Lengths

Mountains and Reefs

Great Barrier Reef, Australia—1,429 mi./2,300 km
This natural wonder is the world's biggest reef and the largest living structure on the planet. Built over centuries by minuscule colonial animals called coral polyps, it is so big, it can be seen from space. It is home to an extraordinary range of sea life, from tiny fish to turtles, rays, sharks, and whales.

Great Himalayan Range, Asia—1,429 mi./2,300 km
The Great Himalayas contain many of the biggest peaks on Earth, including the world's highest, Mount Everest. The mountains were formed some 70 million years ago when two massive tectonic plates collided. According to legend, it is home to the yeti, a giant apelike creature, and in Hindu mythology it is the home of the god Shiva.

Andes Mountains, S. America—5,530 mi./8,900 km
The world's longest mountain chain on land has long been populated by indigenous people, who farm its steep slopes. Today about a third of all the people in South America live in the Andes. Its most famous animal inhabitants include llamas, alpacas, vicuñas, chinchillas, and condors.

Rivers

Yangtze River, China—3,915 mi./6,300 km
The Yangtze River is the longest and busiest river in Asia. Along its course are one of the world's biggest cities (Shanghai), one of the deepest gorges (Tiger Leaping Gorge), and the world's biggest dam (Three Gorges Dam).

Amazon River, S. America—4,000 mi./6,400 km
The Amazon is one of the richest habitats on the planet. It is home to pink dolphins, anacondas, alligators, sloths, and thousands of species of birds and fish. Around one in ten of all known species of wildlife lives in the Amazon River Basin.

Nile River, Africa—4,160 mi./6,695 km
The longest river in the world, the Nile has been an important part of Egyptian life since ancient times. Each spring, the Nile floods, spreading fertile soil around its banks. This soil makes farming possible and brings life to the surrounding desert.

Mid-Ocean Ridge

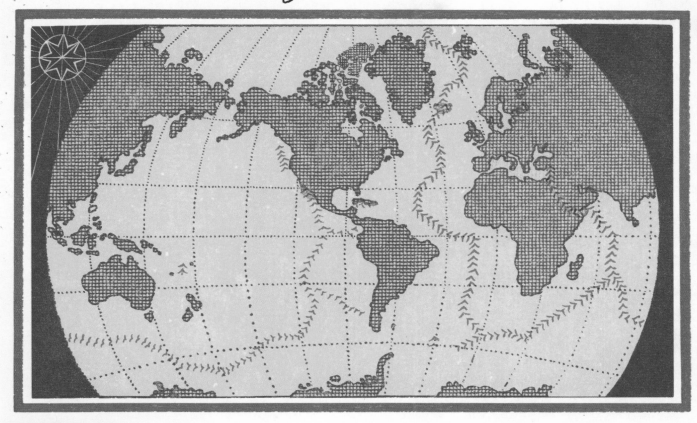

**Mid-Ocean Ridge —
37,282–40,389 mi./
60,000–65,000 km**
The longest and largest mountain range on Earth is hidden from view beneath the ocean. Starting in the Arctic Ocean, the Mid-Ocean Ridge system runs through the Atlantic, past Africa, Asia, Australia, and Antarctica, then across the Pacific to North America. With a total length of around 40,389 mi./65,000 km, it is more than seven times longer than the longest ranges on land.

0 ▬▬▬▬▬ 5,530 mi./8,900 km
The Andes Mountains (the longest mountain range on land)

0 ▬▬▬▬▬▬▬▬▬▬▬▬▬▬▬▬▬▬▬▬▬▬ 40,389 mi./
65,000 km
Mid-Ocean Ridge system (the longest mountain range on Earth)

Human-Made Structures

Trans-Siberian Railway (Moscow to Vladivostok)
Completed: July 21, 1904 | Length—5,753 mi./9,258 km
One of the longest railways in the world, this famous route connects European Russia with the Asian port of Vladivostok, near the border of China. Today it carries millions of passengers and about 110 million tons/100 million metric tons of freight each year.

Great Wall of China
Built c. 259 BCE–1644 CE | Length—13,171 mi./21,196 km
Built to keep northern invaders out of China, the Great Wall is the longest structure ever constructed. It is thought that up to a million people died while building it, and it has been discovered that the mortar used to bind the stones was made with sticky rice.

SPEED on Land and in the Air

Before the invention of planes, trains, and flying machines, people traveled on land no faster than they could ride a galloping horse. When the first steam trains were built, some feared it would be impossible to breathe while moving at such speed or that the vibrations would be so powerful, people might go blind. These fears were soon proved wrong, and ever since, people have striven to reach ever-greater speeds. On May 26, 1969, the Apollo 10 astronauts returning from their moon mission zoomed to Earth at 24,816 miles/39,937 kilometers per hour—around twelve times faster than a rifle bullet and more than thirty times faster than the speed of sound.

FASTER THAN A SPACE SHUTTLE?

When diving through the air, the tiny Anna's hummingbird can fly a mind-boggling 385 body lengths per second (blps). Relative to its size, that's even faster than a space shuttle on reentry into Earth's atmosphere (207 blps).

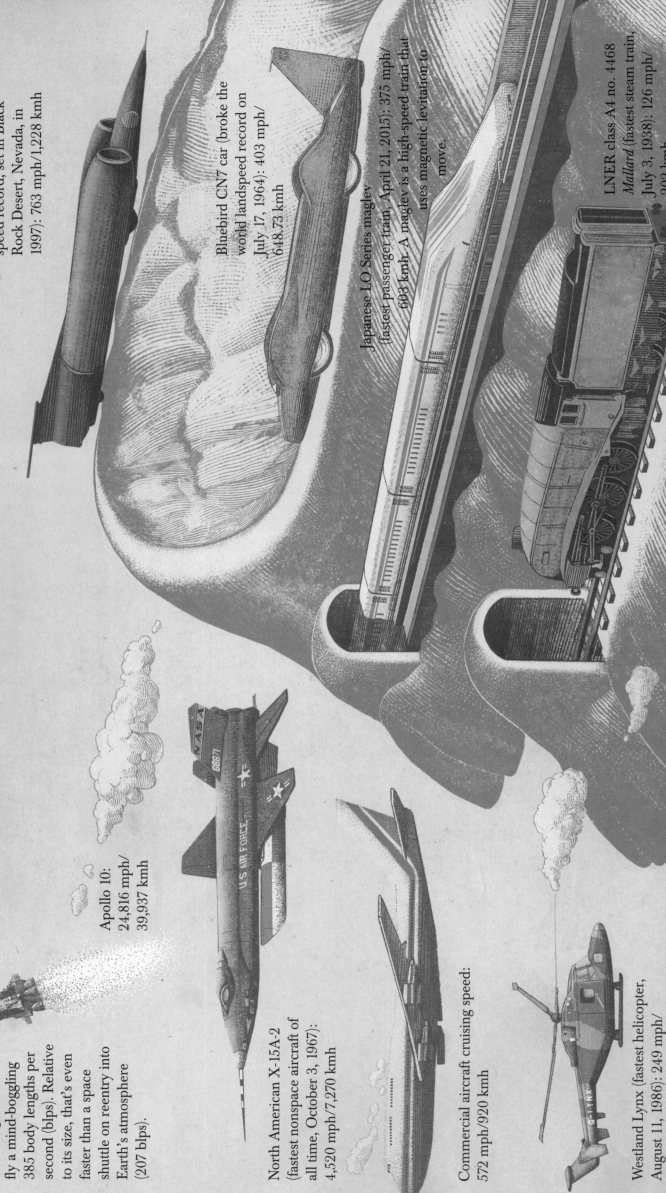

Apollo 10:
24,816 mph/
39,937 kmh

North American X-15A-2 (fastest nonspace aircraft of all time, October 3, 1967):
4,520 mph/7,270 kmh

Commercial aircraft cruising speed:
572 mph/920 kmh

Westland Lynx (fastest helicopter, August 11, 1986): 249 mph/400.87 kmh

Thrust SSC (the current holder of the official land speed record, set in Black Rock Desert, Nevada, in 1997): 763 mph/1,228 kmh

Bluebird CN7 car (broke the world landspeed record on July 17, 1964): 403 mph/648.73 kmh

Japanese LO Series maglev (fastest passenger train, April 21, 2015): 375 mph/603 kmh. A maglev is a high-speed train that uses magnetic levitation to move.

LNER class A4 no. 4468 *Mallard* (fastest steam train, July 3, 1938): 126 mph/202 kmh

Gobron-Brillé
motorcar, 1904:
103 mph/165 kmh

Family car:
70 mph/112 kmh

Cheetah: at
least 60 mph/
95 kmh

Stephenson's
Rocket, 1829:
28 mph/45 kmh

Although they can't
fly, ostriches can run at
speeds of around 45 mph/
72 kmh—faster than
a racehorse.

Benz Patent Motorwagon,
1885–1886 (the world's first
automobile): 10 mph/16 kmh

Peregrine falcon
(when diving):
155 mph/250 kmh

Spirit of St. Louis (flown by
Charles Lindbergh on the first
solo transatlantic flight, in
May 1927): 124 mph/
200 kmh

Hindenburg zeppelin airship:
84 mph/135 kmh

On September 19, 1783,
the Montgolfier brothers
demonstrated their
invention, the hot-air
balloon, to a crowd of
dignitaries. Its first
passengers were a duck,
a rooster, and a sheep named
Montauciel (meaning "climb-
to-the-sky"). The first flight
with human passengers
traveled 5½ mi./9 km and
took 25 minutes: averaging
12 mph/20 kmh.

Wright Flyer, 1903 (the world's first
successful heavier-than-air flying
machine): 10 mph/16 kmh

POWERFUL CREATURES

THE WORLD'S STRONGEST HUMANS

PULL

On July 5, 2017, Reverend Kevin Fast broke his own world record. He pulled a vehicle weighing 109 tons/99 metric tons. That's around 582 times his body weight and equivalent to the combined weight of eight buses, eight compact cars, and five light aircraft.

BACK LIFT

In 1957 it was claimed that Paul Anderson, one of the world's strongest men of all time, back-lifted around 6,261 pounds/2,840 kilograms—the weight of five polar bears.

DEAD LIFT

The world's strongest man in 2016, Eddie Hall, dead-lifted a 1,102-pound/500-kilogram bar above his head—about the weight of a grand piano.

Mammals

For thousands of years, animals have been used for carrying or dragging heavy loads. They have plowed fields, pulled wagons and carts, and transported people across deserts and mountains. But when it comes to brute strength, the African elephant is the strongest of all land animals. A large bull elephant can carry as much as 10 tons/9 metric tons—the weight of around 140 people—and is able to lift logs weighing up to 660 pounds/300 kilograms with its trunk.

BUGS

POWER-LIFTING ANTS

Insects are famed for amazing feats of strength relative to their small size. Some species of ants can lift around fifty times their own body weight using their powerful mandibles (jaws). If humans were as strong as ants, we would be able to lift three family cars above our heads.

THE MIGHTY DUNG BEETLE

Researchers recently discovered a species of dung beetle, *Onthophagus taurus*, that can pull 1,141 times its own body weight. That's nearly equivalent to a person pulling four whale sharks. This super strength makes these beetles excellent diggers and dung rollers.

WORLD'S STRONGEST

One of the strongest animals of all is not actually an insect but rather a species of mite called *Archegozetes longisetosus*. It is only 1 millimeter long, but it can hold 1,180 times its weight using its tiny claws. Imagine carrying around nine elephants and you'll have some idea of what this mighty mite can do.

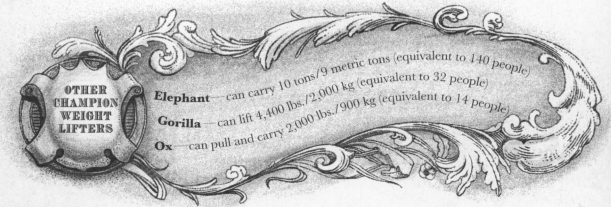

OTHER CHAMPION WEIGHT LIFTERS

Elephant—can carry 10 tons/9 metric tons (equivalent to 140 people)

Gorilla—can lift 4,400 lbs./2,000 kg (equivalent to 32 people)

Ox—can pull and carry 2,000 lbs./900 kg (equivalent to 14 people)

DEATHLY GRIP OF THE TITANOBOA

Powerful Jumpers

Slithering through the hot, swampy jungles of South America around 58 million years ago, the 46-foot-/14-meter-long *Titanoboa* was one of the most powerful predators of its day. Like modern boas, it killed its prey by squeezing it to death. Scientists have estimated that it constricted its victims with a force of 398 pounds per square inch/28 kilograms per square centimeter and a total force of up to 660 tons/600 metric tons—the equivalent of being crushed under the weight of almost ten tanks!

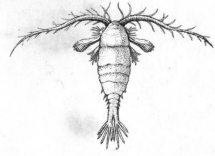

Thanks to their tiny but extra-powerful leg muscles, copepods can "jump" through the water at a speed of 300 to 1,000 body lengths per second. That's equivalent to a 5½-foot-/1.7-meter-tall person leaping around 5,600 feet/1,700 meters in one second.

Winged Creatures

TIGER OF THE SKIES

With its large legs and talons as big as a tiger's claws, the Haast's eagle, which went extinct around 1400, was one of the most powerful birds that ever lived. It preyed on much bigger flightless birds such as the giant moa, crushing the moa's pelvis with its feet. Experts say it may even have been capable of swooping down and killing a small child.

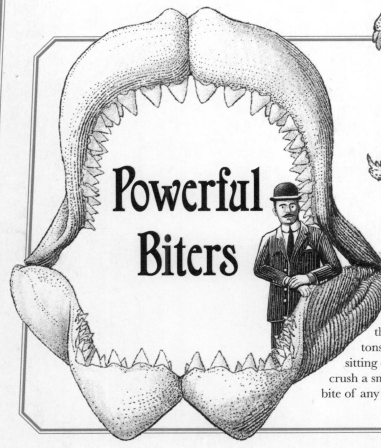

Powerful Biters

With an estimated bite force of more than 5½ **tons**/5 metric tons, the fearsome *T. rex* was the most powerful biter of any land animal. But that is nothing compared to the megalodon, which lived in ancient oceans around 16 million years ago. It is thought that these giant sharks could close their jaws around their prey with a force of about 20 tons/18 metric tons. That's equivalent to four medium-size elephants sitting down on the ground and powerful enough to crush a small car. The saltwater crocodile has the strongest bite of any animal alive today (around 3,700 lbs./1,600 kg).

AFRICAN CROWNED EAGLE

One of the strongest birds alive today, the crowned eagle can kill animals more than four times its own body weight.

SNAPPING CLAWS OF THE PISTOL SHRIMP

This feisty crustacean can snap its claws shut with such force that it creates a shock wave that can knock out its prey. The blast is so powerful that some species use it to drill into solid rock, and the sound it makes is so loud that it can interfere with ships' sonar.

HOW HEAVY?
NATURAL WORLD

OSTRICH EGG
WEIGHT: 3 lbs./1.4 kg

Ostriches lay the largest eggs of all living birds. One egg can weigh as much as twenty-four chicken eggs or two basketballs.

AFRICAN ELEPHANT
WEIGHT: 6.61 tons/6 metric tons

The biggest land mammal—the African elephant—weighs the same as around one hundred people.

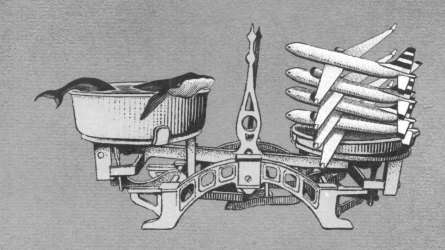

SUMO WRESTLER
WEIGHT: 584 lbs./265 kg

Weighing more than four times an average person, Ryūichi Yamamoto is thought to be the heaviest Japanese sumo wrestler of all time. Sumo wrestlers reach their gargantuan size by eating vast quantities of *chankonabe*, a type of Japanese stew.

BLUE WHALE
WEIGHT: up to 200 tons/180 metric tons | tongue: 4½ tons/ 4 metric tons | heart: 400–1,500 lbs./180–680 kg

The blue whale is the heaviest animal on Earth; it can grow to weigh more than four Boeing 737 planes, its tongue can weigh as much as an elephant, and its heart as much as a small car. It feeds by taking in massive gulps of seawater full of krill, but despite its size, it can't swallow anything bigger than a beach ball.

CREATURES THEN & NOW

One of the heaviest creatures ever to have stomped the Earth, the *Argentinosaurus*, weighed around ten times more than the mighty T. rex. *The blue whale, however, is around two times heavier than the biggest dinosaurs and weighs more than thirty African elephants.*

Blue whale

Argentinosaurus huinculensis

African elephant

Tyrannosaurus rex

Stegosaurus

White rhinoceros

Common hippopotamus

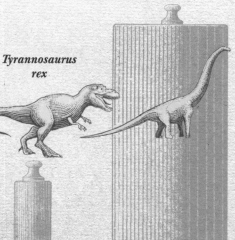

Stegosaurus	White rhinoceros	Common hippopotamus	African elephant	Tyrannosaurus rex	Argentinosaurus	Blue whale
4 tons/ 3.6 metric tons	4 tons/ 3.6 metric tons	4 tons/ 3.6 metric tons	6½ tons/ 6 metric tons	6½ tons/ 6 metric tons	55 tons/ 50 metric tons	200 tons/ 180 metric tons

THE WEIGHT OF THE WORLD

Scientists have concluded that Earth's mass is approximately

**6,600,000,000,000,000,000,000,000 tons/
6,600,000,000,000,000,000,000,000
metric tons.**

So, when we build really big things—a skyscraper, an oil tanker, or a space rocket—do we make Earth heavier? The answer is no. Humans and things are made with the matter that is already in or on the planet. All we're doing is simply moving atoms from one place on Earth to another.

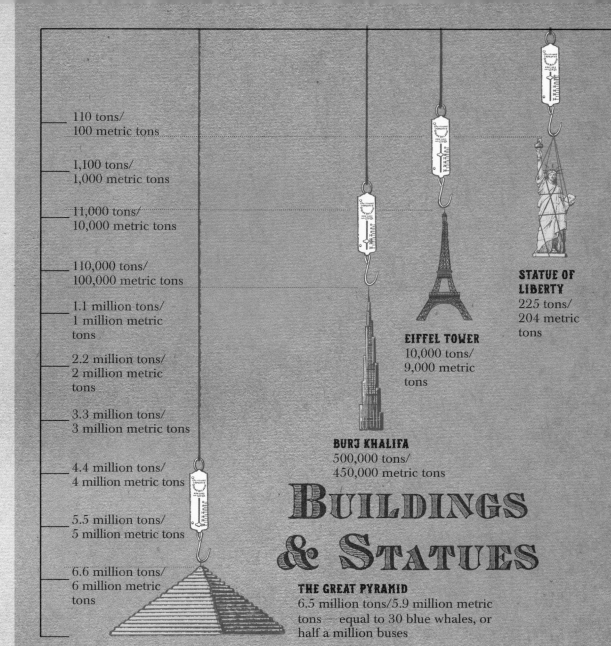

- 110 tons/100 metric tons
- 1,100 tons/1,000 metric tons
- 11,000 tons/10,000 metric tons
- 110,000 tons/100,000 metric tons
- 1.1 million tons/1 million metric tons
- 2.2 million tons/2 million metric tons
- 3.3 million tons/3 million metric tons
- 4.4 million tons/4 million metric tons
- 5.5 million tons/5 million metric tons
- 6.6 million tons/6 million metric tons

STATUE OF LIBERTY
225 tons/204 metric tons

EIFFEL TOWER
10,000 tons/9,000 metric tons

BURJ KHALIFA
500,000 tons/450,000 metric tons

BUILDINGS & STATUES

THE GREAT PYRAMID
6.5 million tons/5.9 million metric tons—equal to 30 blue whales, or half a million buses

PYRAMIDS & MEGALITHS

Carved from stone hundreds and thousands of years ago, enormous monuments can be found in many countries around the world. Each giant stone had to be transported—sometimes hundreds of miles— before being heaved into position. Exactly how our ancestors managed to carry out these amazing engineering feats remains a mystery to this day.

GREAT PYRAMID OF GIZA, EGYPT
Built: c. 2580–2560 BCE
Each stone block: 3–16½ tons/2.5–15 metric tons

STONEHENGE, WILTSHIRE, ENGLAND
Built: c. 3000–2500 BCE
Heaviest stone: 28–33 tons/25–30 metric tons

EASTER ISLAND STATUES, CHILE
Built: c. 1100–1600 CE
Heaviest moai (statue): 81½ tons/74 metric tons

BUSES & SHIPS

The average bus weighs around 12 tons/11 metric tons—the same as about three hippos.

One of the most famous ships ever built—RMS *Titanic*—weighed more than 50,706 tons/46,000 metric tons and was the biggest movable structure of its day. Scientists believe the mega-iceberg that sank the ship had a mass of around 1.7 million tons/1.5 million metric tons.

HUMAN HISTORY *in a* Week

If we were to condense all of human history so far into a SINGLE WEEK—with the first Homo sapiens arriving in the first second of the first day—the Ancient Egyptian civilization would last just 2½ hours and Neil Armstrong would take his first steps on the moon at 2½ minutes to midnight on the final day.

DAY 7
19:49

3000 BCE

c. 3300 BCE
Invention of writing in Sumer, Mesopotamia

c. 3000–2500 BCE
Stonehenge—a giant stone monument—is built using simple Bronze Age tools.

c. 3000–30 BCE
ANCIENT EGYPTIAN CIVILIZATION

c. 3300–600 BCE
BRONZE AGE
People start using bronze to make tools, weapons, armor, and jewelry.

c. 3300–1700 BCE
INDUS VALLEY CIVILIZATION
One of the oldest civilizations. Hinduism probably has its roots in the Indus Valley.

c. 4000–330 BCE
ANCIENT MESOPOTAMIA
One of the earliest great civilizations. The first ancient cities are built here.

c. 2580–2560 BCE
The Great Pyramids are built.

c. 1200–500 BC
Start of THE IRON AGE

DAY 7
21:29

1000 BCE

c. 566–410 BCE
Life of Buddha and birth of Buddhism

DAY 7
20:39

2000 BCE

c. 1600–1046 BCE
CHINESE SHANG DYNASTY
The first recorded Chinese dynasty. The earliest examples of Chinese writing are from this period.

c. 1100–146 BCE
ANCIENT GREECE
The ancient Greeks are famous for being great warriors, poets, politicians, and philosophers.

c. 776 BCE
The first-ever Olympic games are held in honor of the Greek god Zeus.

753 BCE–476 CE
ANCIENT ROME
At their most powerful, the Romans ruled over much of Europe, North Africa, and Asia.

DAY 7
23:34

1500

DAY 7
23:39

1600

1596
The first flush toilet is invented by John Harington.

1532
The Incan Empire is conquered by the conquistador Francisco Pizzaro González.

1519–1521 • The mighty Aztec Empire is conquered by Hernán Cortés, a Spanish conquistador (soldier and explorer), who had come to the Americas in search of gold.

1492
Christopher Columbus voyages to the Americas.

1440
Invention of the printing press by Johannes Gutenberg

1405–1433
Zhang He, a Ming dynasty admiral, sails to Asia and Africa, bringing back all kinds of exotic objects, including pearls, spices, camels, zebras, and giraffes.

THE LAST 10 MINUTES

DAY 7
23:44

1700

1789
French Revolution

DAY 7
23:49

1800

1608
Invention of the telescope by Hans Lippershey

1620 • English pilgrims aboard the *Mayflower* arrive at Cape Cod.

c. 1680–1820
THE AGE OF ENLIGHTENMENT

1776
American Independence declared

1800s • INDUSTRIAL REVOLUTION
The manufacturing of goods moves from small shops and homes to large factories. Many people move from the countryside to cities, and new technologies and types of transportation are introduced.

DAY 1
00:00:01

c. 200,000 YEARS AGO
First modern humans
(*Homo sapiens*)

DAY 7
16:30

9000 BC

DAY 6
23:00

30,000 BCE

DAYS 1-6

c. 9000–3300 BCE • NEOLITHIC ERA
People begin to live in settlements and learn how to grow crops. The first animals are domesticated for their milk, meat, and hides. Farming tools, pottery, and weaving are developed.

c. 31,000–28,000 BCE
Some of the earliest known examples of rock art

c. 200,000–9000 BCE
Early humans live a nomadic lifestyle, scavenging or hunting such wild animals as saber-tooth tigers and woolly mammoths. Stone tools are used for hunting, fishing, building shelters, and making clothes.

THE LAST HOUR

DAY 7
22:19

1 CE

c. 570 CE
Birth of Mohammed and the rise of Islam

DAY 7
23:09

1000

c. 206 BCE
Invention of the magnetic compass in ancient China

c. 4 BCE–30 CE
Life of Jesus

c. 80 CE
Thousands of gladiators and animals are killed in the three-month-long inaugural games at the Roman Colosseum.

c. 105 CE
Invention of papermaking in ancient China

c. 250–900 CE
MAYAN CIVILIZATION

c. 476–1500 CE
MIDDLE AGES

c. 800 CE
Gunpowder is invented by the Chinese.

c. 800–1050 CE
THE VIKING AGE
The Vikings sail all over Europe and to the Americas in their longboats. Some raid villages and kill the local people. Others settle as farmers, fishermen, and craftsmen.

DAY 7
23:29

1400

c. 1350–1600s
RENAISSANCE & THE AGE OF DISCOVERY

DAY 7
23:24

1300

1368–1644
MING DYNASTY
The Chinese Ming finish the Great Wall and build a huge palace called the Forbidden City.

Art, literature, and new ideas about mathematics, philosophy, and science flourish. Nations explore the world and discover new trade routes.

1347–1351
The Black Death kills around a third of the population of Europe.

c. 1325–1521
AZTEC EMPIRE
A powerful nation of warriors known for carrying out human sacrifices

c. 1200–1532 • INCAN EMPIRE
The Incas worship the sun god Inti and make many beautiful golden objects. According to legends, the emperor of Cuzco built an entire city with temples, buildings, plants, and trees all made of gold.

DAY 7
23:59

2000

1903 • The world's first heavier-than-air flying machine

DAY 7
23:54

1900

1885–1886
The first automobile

1914–1918
World War I

1939–1945 • World War II.
1945: The first atomic bomb is dropped, on the city of Hiroshima.

1969
The first person on the moon

PRESENT DAY
Rovers are sent to Mars to look for signs of life.

65

History of the Universe

If the whole lifetime of the universe were compressed into a single year, modern humans wouldn't arrive until eight minutes to midnight on December 31. The past four hundred years would pass in the blink of an eye, and a single human life would last just a fraction of a second.

The calendar begins with the Big Bang on January 1 . . .

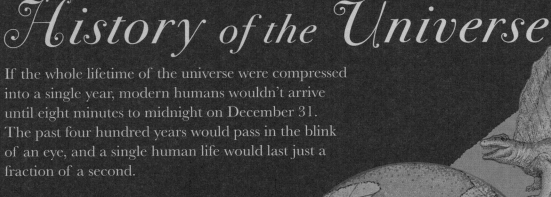

JANUARY

January 1, 12 am—The Big Bang (c. 13.7 bya)

January 1, 12:15 am—The first neutrons form (400,000 years after the Big Bang).

January 19—First stars and galaxies begin to form (c. 13 bya).

FEBRUARY

MARCH

APRIL

MAY

May 11—Milky Way galaxy is formed (c. 8.8 bya)

JUNE

JULY

AUGUST

SEPTEMBER

September 1—Birth of our sun (c. 4.6 bya) and the formation of our solar system (c. 4.56 bya)

September 22—First simple life on Earth (prokaryotes) (c. 3.8 bya)

OCTOBER

October 1–26—Photosynthesis and oxygenation of atmosphere (c. 3.5–2.5 bya)

NOVEMBER

November 9—First cells with internal organs develop on Earth (c. 2 bya)

DECEMBER

December 11–17—First multicellular life and simple animals: sponges, jellyfish, sea anemones and corals (c. 800–580 mya)

December 18—First vertebrates (creatures with backbones) and trilobites, the first hard-bodied animals (c. 520 mya)

December 19—First insects (c. 479 mya) and first nonvascular land plants (without roots, stems, or leaves) (c. 470 mya)

December 20—First vascular plants (c. 430 mya) and first fish with jaws, such as *Entelognathus* (c. 419 mya)

December 21—First flying insects (c. 400 mya) and first trees (c. 380 mya). As plants grow taller, insects develop flight. By 300 million years ago, there are species of damselflies as big as a seagull.

December 22—First amphibians (c. 360 mya). Animals develop adaptations for living on land as well as in water.

December 23—First reptiles (c. 312 mya). Animals, such as the lizardlike *Hylonomus*, evolve to live entirely on dry land.

December 24—Mammal-like reptiles such as the bizarre-looking *Edaphosaurus* begin to thrive on land. They have clawed

feet, sharp teeth, and large sails on their backs (c. 300–288 mya).

December 24–25—The continents join into a supercontinent called Pangaea, allowing animals to roam more freely (c. 299–272 mya).

December 26—The first dinosaurs evolve from reptiles (c. 230 mya). Early types include the plant-eating *Plateosaurus*.

December 27–28—Jurassic period (c. 201–145 mya). The high point of the dinosaurs. Species include *Allosaurus*, *Stegosaurus*, and *Diplodocus*.

December 27—First true mammals (c. 160 mya). The earliest known placental mammals, such as the *Juramaia*, are small and shrewlike.

December 28—First birds evolve from small carnivorous dinosaurs (c. 150 mya).

December 28–30—Cretaceous period (c. 145–66 mya). The age of the giant dinosaurs and pterosaurs, including *Tyrannosaurus, Argentinosaurus, Triceratops, Iguanodon,* and *Quetzalcoatlus* continues.

December 28—First flowers (c. 130 mya). Thought to be one of the most

December
23

December
24

September
22

December
14

December
24–25

December
26

December
17

January
1

December
18

December
27–28

December
27

December
22

December
21

December
31

December
30

September
1

May
11

December
20

December
19

December
28–30

December
28

On this scale:
Each day = 37.5 million years
Each hour = 1.56 million years
Each minute = 26,000 years
Each second = 434 years

important moments in the history of life on Earth. Green forests become filled with color, and new species of insects, birds, and animals flourish.

December 30—At 00:01 a huge asteroid or comet collides with Earth, causing the mass extinction of 65–75 percent of all species, including all non-bird dinosaurs and marine reptiles (c. 66 mya). Mammals diversify and at about 16:00 the first mammals, such as the *Ambulocetus* (or "walking whale"), take to the seas (c. 50 mya).

THE LAST DAY — December 31
Mammals continue to diversify on land and at sea and reach enormous sizes (giraffes, mammoths, whales).

18:54—Expansion of grasslands around the world (c. 8–3 mya)
20:10—First human-like apes (c. 6 mya)
21:26—Early hominids first walk upright on two legs (c. 4 mya).
22:24—Ice Age begins, first use of stone tools, rise of megafauna (c. 2.5 mya)
23:52—*Homo sapiens* (c. 200,000 ya)

23.57—Human migration around the world (c. 80,000 ya)
23.59—Early cave paintings (c. 33,000 ya)

THE LAST MINUTE
23:59:33—End of Ice Age (c. 11,600 ya)
23:59:33—Farming begins (c. 10,000 ya)
23:59:45—Wheel invented (c. 5,500 ya)
23:59:48—Stonehenge built (c. 5,000 ya)
23:59:49—Great Pyramids (c. 4,500 ya)
23:59:55—Colosseum built (c. 2,000 ya)
23:59:58—Columbus sails to the Americas (c. 525 ya)

THE LAST SECOND
In the last second, humankind has invented the telescope, the microscope, and the first flush toilet. We have built palaces and skyscrapers; discovered penicillin and cured diseases; invented cars, trains, planes, the telephone, and the Internet. We have had revolutions and wars, dropped atomic bombs, put a person on the moon, and sent probes to Mars!

ya = years ago • mya = million years ago • bya = billion years ago

Small Creatures

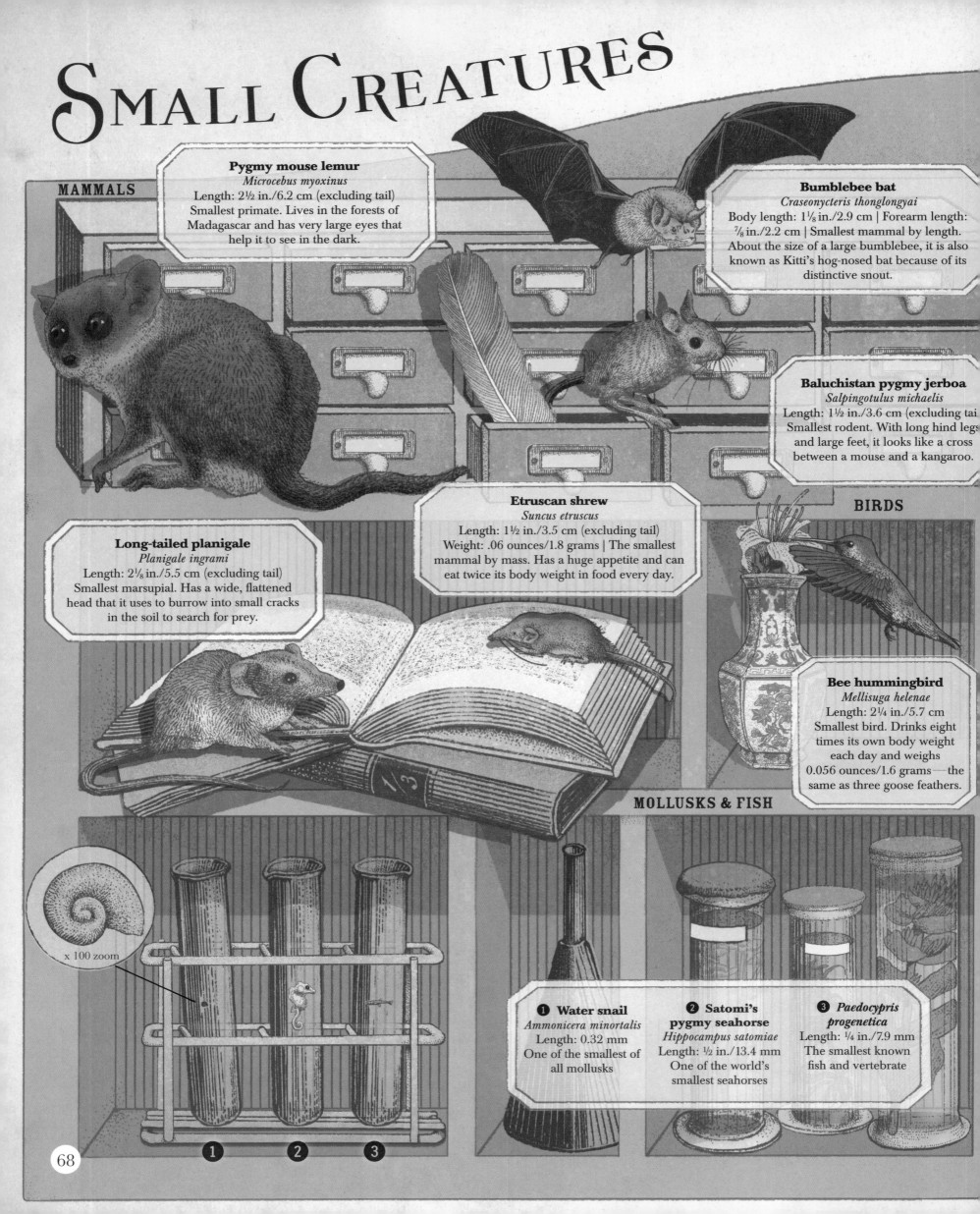

MAMMALS

Pygmy mouse lemur
Microcebus myoxinus
Length: 2½ in./6.2 cm (excluding tail)
Smallest primate. Lives in the forests of Madagascar and has very large eyes that help it to see in the dark.

Bumblebee bat
Craseonycteris thonglongyai
Body length: 1⅛ in./2.9 cm | Forearm length: ⅞ in./2.2 cm | Smallest mammal by length. About the size of a large bumblebee, it is also known as Kitti's hog-nosed bat because of its distinctive snout.

Baluchistan pygmy jerboa
Salpingotulus michaelis
Length: 1½ in./3.6 cm (excluding tail)
Smallest rodent. With long hind legs and large feet, it looks like a cross between a mouse and a kangaroo.

Etruscan shrew
Suncus etruscus
Length: 1½ in./3.5 cm (excluding tail)
Weight: .06 ounces/1.8 grams | The smallest mammal by mass. Has a huge appetite and can eat twice its body weight in food every day.

BIRDS

Long-tailed planigale
Planigale ingrami
Length: 2⅛ in./5.5 cm (excluding tail)
Smallest marsupial. Has a wide, flattened head that it uses to burrow into small cracks in the soil to search for prey.

Bee hummingbird
Mellisuga helenae
Length: 2¼ in./5.7 cm
Smallest bird. Drinks eight times its own body weight each day and weighs 0.056 ounces/1.6 grams—the same as three goose feathers.

MOLLUSKS & FISH

x 100 zoom

❶ Water snail
Ammonicera minortalis
Length: 0.32 mm
One of the smallest of all mollusks

❷ Satomi's pygmy seahorse
Hippocampus satomiae
Length: ½ in./13.4 mm
One of the world's smallest seahorses

❸ *Paedocypris progenetica*
Length: ¼ in./7.9 mm
The smallest known fish and vertebrate

❶   ❷   ❸

REPTILES, AMPHIBIANS & BUTTERFLIES

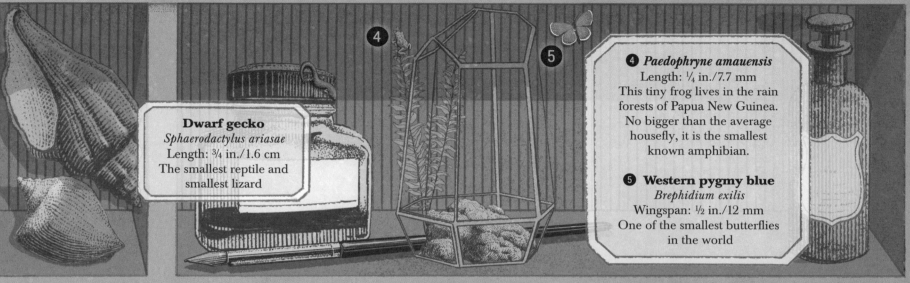

Dwarf gecko
Sphaerodactylus ariasae
Length: ¾ in./1.6 cm
The smallest reptile and
smallest lizard

4 *Paedophryne amauensis*
Length: ¼ in./7.7 mm
This tiny frog lives in the rain
forests of Papua New Guinea.
No bigger than the average
housefly, it is the smallest
known amphibian.

5 **Western pygmy blue**
Brephidium exilis
Wingspan: ½ in./12 mm
One of the smallest butterflies
in the world

MICROORGANISMS

Microorganisms are
so small that we can
see them only with
a microscope. They
live all around us—
in the soil, in the
oceans, in the air, on
our skin, and inside
our bodies. Many are
harmless, but some
are deadly.

6 **Fairyfly** *or* **Fairy wasp**
Dicopomorpha echmepterygis
Length: 139 microns
A parasitic wasp that lives inside
the eggs of other insects. Smallest
known insect.

Diatoms (various species)
Length: Typically 2–500 microns
Microscopic algae that live in nearly every habitat where water is found.
They are eaten by all kinds of animals, from tiny microorganisms to fish and
whales. Hundreds of them could fit on a grain of sand.

x 100 zoom

7 *Pelagibacter ubique*
Length: 0.37–0.89 microns
One of the smallest free-living
bacteria. More than five thousand of
them could fit on a grain of sand.

x 50,000 zoom

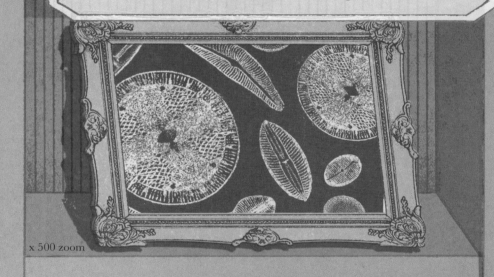

x 500 zoom

HOW SMALL IS AN ATOM?

Everything in the universe — from
the tallest tower to the smallest
microorganism — is made up of tiny
things called atoms. They are the
building blocks of all matter, and they
are very, very small. They are around a
million times smaller than the thickest
human hair and are so small that if the
atoms in an apple were enlarged to
the size of an apple, the apple itself
would be as big as Earth.

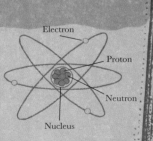

Electron

Proton

Neutron

Nucleus

Radius of a typical atom:
100 picometers

Stars and Galaxies

STARS

Stars come in all different sizes and colors, from red dwarfs and neutron stars to blue and red supergiants—the biggest stars in the universe. Our star—the Sun—is at the center of our Solar System. Without its heat and light, no life could survive on Earth.

Giant Stars

Our sun is the largest object in our solar system, but compared with some stars, it is no bigger than a fleck of dust. The biggest stars in the universe are the monster red supergiants—dying stars that have bloated to many times their original size. Eventually they will explode and become neutron stars or black holes.

Smallest Stars

(The measurements in parentheses are solar radii. 1 R = the radius of the sun)

Rigel
(blue supergiant)
Radius: 33.7 million mi./
54.3 million km (78 R)
Blue supergiants are the hottest and brightest stars in the universe. Rigel is more than seventy times bigger than the sun and emits 60,000 times more light.

Sun

Pollux
(red giant)
Radius:
3.8 million mi./
6.1 million km (8.8 R)
As a star like our sun runs out of fuel, it grows bigger and redder, turning into a red giant. Eventually it will collapse and become a white dwarf.

Sun
(main sequence star)
Radius: 432,288 mi./695,700 km
Our sun is a main sequence star—one of the most common types of stars. It is fueled through nuclear fusion; as its hydrogen atoms crash together, they become helium and produce energy.

Rigel

Betelgeuse
(red supergiant)
Radius: 510 million mi./ 821 million km
(1,180 R)
This supergiant is more than a thousand times wider than our sun.

Around Earth by rocket: 1 hour

2MASS Jo523-1403
(red dwarf star)
Radius: 37,177 mi./59,830 km
(0.086 R)
Red dwarfs are main sequence stars like our sun but are smaller and cooler.

Jupiter
Radius: 42,944 mi./69,911 km
(0.1 R)
The biggest planet in our solar system

Earth
Radius: 3,959 mi./
6,371 km (0.009 R)

Neutron star
(Not visible on this scale)
Measuring as little as 12 mi./
20 km across, neutron stars are the smallest stars known to exist.

Sirius B (white dwarf star)
Radius: 3,631 mi./5,844 km
(0.0084 R)
As an average star like our sun dies, it becomes a white dwarf—a small, hot, and very dense star.

UY Scuti
(red supergiant)
Radius: 735 million mi./1.1 billion km (1,700 R)
The biggest known star by radius is more than 1,700 times the size of the sun. If Earth were shrunk to the size of a marble, the sun would be the size of a child and UY Scuti would be taller than two Burj Khalifas.

Death of a Star

As a massive star nears the end of its life, it explodes as a supernova — an explosion so big that it briefly shines more brightly than an entire galaxy.

A star that is born eight to twenty times more massive than the sun ends its life as a neutron star.

As it explodes, the star's core is squashed down into a tiny compact ball known as a neutron star. It is so dense that one cubic centimeter might weigh around 1.1 billion tons/1 billion metric tons. That's the mass of Mount Everest, but squeezed into a space the size of a sugar cube.

A star that is born at least twenty times more massive than the sun ends its life as a black hole.

The star's core is compressed into a space no bigger than an atom, and its gravitational pull is so strong that nothing can escape it — not even light.

GALAXIES

Until a hundred or so years ago, few people imagined that anything existed beyond our galaxy, the Milky Way. We now know that it is just one of billions of galaxies in the universe. Some are very small. Others are much, much bigger than our own.

Galaxies Compared

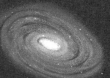

Messier 33
(spiral galaxy)
Diameter:
50,000 light-years

Across the Milky Way by rocket: 2.7 billion years

Milky Way
(spiral galaxy)
Diameter:
100,000 light-years
There are around
200 billion stars in
the Milky Way.

Andromeda
(spiral galaxy)
Diameter: 220,000 light-years
Our nearest galaxy. Andromeda is expected to collide with the Milky Way in around 4.6 billion years to form a giant elliptical galaxy.

To the Edge of the Universe

Scientists have estimated that the observable universe — in other words, the part that we can see — has a diameter of 93 billion light-years. Our Milky Way would fit inside it 10 quintillion times.

Across the known universe by rocket: 2.5 quadrillion years

Milky Way

IC11-01
(supergiant elliptical galaxy)
Diameter: 6 million light-years
Over billions of years, galaxies have collided and merged to form this supergalaxy. It is around fifty times wider than the Milky Way and may contain as many as 100 trillion stars. At its center is a supermassive black hole.

How Big Is the Universe?

So how big is the entire universe? No one really knows if the universe stretches on forever, or even if ours is the only universe that exists.

Selected Bibliography

Books

Burnie, David, and Don E. Wilson, editors. *Animal: The Definitive Visual Guide*. 3rd ed. New York: DK, 2017.

Ocean: The Definitive Visual Guide. Rev. ed. New York: DK, 2014.

Paul, Gregory S. *The Princeton Field Guide to Dinosaurs*. 2nd ed. Princeton, NJ: Princeton University Press, 2016.

Websites

All About Birds
www.allaboutbirds.org

Animal Diversity Web
https://animaldiversity.org

Atlas Obscura
www.atlasobscura.com

Australian Museum
https://australianmuseum.net.au

Bio Kids: Kids' Inquiry of Diverse Species
www.biokids.umich.edu

ButterflyCorner.net
https://en.butterflycorner.net

Earthguide
earthguide.uscd.edu

Encyclopedia Britannica
www.britannica.com

Entomology Today
https://entomologytoday.org

Mass Audubon
www.massaudubon.org

NASA
www.nasa.gov

National Geographic
www.nationalgeographic.com/animals/index/

National Oceanic and Atmospheric Administration
www.noaa.gov

National Park Service
www.nps.gov/index.htm

National Weather Service
www.weather.gov

Natural Worlds
www.naturalworlds.org

Nepal.com
www.nepal.com

Northern Lights Centre
www.northernlightscentre.ca/northernlights.html

Oceana
https://oceana.org

Phys.org
https://phys.org

Rocky Mountain Tree-Ring Research
www.rmtrr.org

The Royal Society for the Protection of Birds
www.rspb.org.uk

Sharkopedia
https://sharkopedia.discovery.com

Sloth Sanctuary Cost Rica
www.slothsanctuary.com

Smithsonian
www.si.edu

Smithsonian National Air and Space Museum
https://airandspace.si.edu

Smithsonian National Museum of Natural History
Global Volcanism Program
https://volcano.si.edu

Smithsonian National Zoo and Conservation Biology Institute
https://nationalzoo.si.edu

South African National Parks
www.sanparks.org/parks/

Space.com
www.space.com

SummitPost.org
www.summitpost.org

ToursOption: Derinkuyu Underground City
http://turkey.toursoption.com/Historic-Sites/
Derinkuyu-Underground-City-Derinkuyu-Koyu-
Pl41/?lang=en

UNESCO
https://en.unesco.org

United States Parachute Association
https://uspa.org

U.S. Fish and Wildlife Service
www.fws.gov

Vermont Fish and Wildlife
www.vtfishandwildlife.com

Wildscreen Arkive
www.arkive.org

World Wildlife Fund
www.worldwildlife.org

Weather Underground
www.wunderground.com

Glossary

Age of Enlightenment
A period from about 1680 to 1820 during which many new political and scientific ideas arose

aurora borealis
A spectacular display of swirling, colored light in the sky seen near the North Pole. It's produced by particles from the sun hitting the top of Earth's atmosphere.

bacteria
Very tiny living things with just a single cell

baleen whale
A whale with a filter system in its mouth rather than teeth, which it uses to capture tiny creatures from seawater as food

biomass
The total quantity of living things

bongo
A type of African forest antelope that is active at night

carnivore
An animal that eats other animals

cell
The smallest component of a living thing. All living things are made up of cells.

chinchilla
A rodent from South America that looks rather like a ground squirrel, with a long furry tail

clonal colony
A collection of plants that have grown from a single plant by cloning. Often, new plants grow up from roots of the original. They are all genetically identical (clones).

comet
A lump of dust and ice that orbits the sun. When it is close to the sun, part of the ice melts and forms a long tail that streams out of the comet and is lit up by sunlight.

copepod
A type of small crustacean that lives in freshwater or seawater all around the world

Cree
A group of North American First People living in Canada

crises
Emergency situations

crustacean
An animal with a hard outer shell, a body in segments, and often with jointed legs. Many crustaceans live in water.

decibel
A unit used to measure the volume of a sound

diversify
Become more varied

elixir
A liquid intended as a medicine or magical potion

elliptical
In the shape of an ellipse, or oval

fertile
With plentiful nutrients needed by growing plants

hemisphere
Half of a sphere; the Earth is divided into Northern and Southern hemispheres, as well as into Eastern and Western Hemispheres

herbivore
An animal that eats plants

hibernation
A resting state in which some animals spend the winter months

hominids
Modern and earlier forms of humans

host
The animal or plant in which a parasite, bacterium, or virus lives

hydrothermal vent
The opening in the seabed that pours out hot water rich in chemicals

immortality
The state of living forever

larval
The condition of being a larva, an immature form such as a caterpillar or maggot

lichen
Complex plantlike organisms, consisting of an alga or cyanobacterium and a fungus; they grow on trees and rocks

magma
Scorching hot, semi-liquid molten rock within the Earth

magnetic levitation
A process by which objects are held up in the air and propelled forward by the force of repelling magnets

Maori
The first people of New Zealand, originally from Polynesia

megafauna
Very large animals

mortar
A cement-like mixture that holds bricks or stone blocks together in a building; also a small bowl in which substances are pounded with a pestle

mummified
Preserved by being dried out, either deliberately or by environmental conditions

mya
Million years ago

nematode
A very simple type of worm. There are many different types of nematodes that live in all kinds of environments.

neutron
A tiny particle with no electrical charge in the nucleus (center) of an atom

nomadic
Following a lifestyle that involves having no fixed residence but rather moving from place to place, often over a route that repeats each year

non-clonal
Not clonal; in clonal reproduction, offspring are an exact genetic copy of the parent

opalescent
Reflecting or displaying various colors

organisms
Living things, including plants, animals, and microbes

oxygenation
The process of the gas oxygen being added to a substance

parasitic
Living on and feeding from a plant or animal while it is still alive

pedestal
A base or support

Permian
Prehistoric period from 299 to 252 million years ago

petrified
Turned to stone

philosopher
A person who examines, reflects on, and analyzes fundamental concepts and ideas

photosynthesis
A process by which green plants make the sugar glucose from oxygen in the atmosphere and water from the soil, powered by the energy in sunlight

plankton
Very small living creatures in the sea or freshwater, including bacteria, algae, and tiny animals

polyp (coral)
A tiny organism that produces a hard casing around its base and has a soft body above with tentacles. Polyps clone to make large colonies, forming coral.

polyp (jellyfish)
A stage in the life of a jellyfish when it is attached by a stalk to a solid object, ending with a mouth surrounded by tentacles

predator
An animal that preys on other animals for food

prokaryote
The simplest form of organism, with a single cell of the simplest type

reptile
A cold-blooded vertebrate that breathes with lungs. Most reptiles lay eggs.

scavenging
Searching for dead animals to eat

species
Genetically distinct types of organisms

tectonic plate
A slab of the Earth's crust that carries continental land or ocean and sits on top of the magma of the mantle. The tectonic plates move extremely slowly around the Earth.

Ten Commandments
According to the Bible, a set of ethical rules revealed to the prophet Moses

terrestrial
On land

trilobite
An extinct sea creature with a jointed body that lived 521 to 252 million years ago

vegetatively cloned
Reproduced by being grown from a part of a plant (such as a cutting or root), resulting in an exact genetic copy of the parent plant

vertebrate
An animal with a backbone

vicuña
South American animal related to the camel that lives in the high mountains of the Andes

vocalization
Making a noise with a voice

A Note from the Artist

Ever since I was a child, science books have fascinated me because the illustrations are so incredibly detailed. Even now that I'm older, I'm still very fond of them.

I have been collecting vintage items since my university days. In fact, there's a huge German science chart from the 1930s hanging on the wall of my studio. These images take me back to a time without technology and make me feel sentimental. I am drawn to the exquisite beauty of traditional craftsmanship, an affinity that is often reflected in the colors and fine line of my own artwork.

I hope this book inspires you — just as my own books inspired me when I was a child.

Page Tsou